From a small farm in New Jersey
to the shores of Okinawa...

Contents

Chapter 1

Early Days 5

Chapter 2

Growing Up in York, Pennsylvania 14

Chapter 3

The First Island – Boot Camp 25

Chapter 4

Marine Aviation Ordnance School – Norman, Oklahoma 31

Chapter 5

Marine Aviation Squadrons VMTB 143 and 232 -- Santa Barbara, California 34

Chapter 6

Across the Wide Pacific 37

Chapter 7

The New Hebrides 41

Chapter 8

The Big Lagoon 47

Chapter 9

Sailing into the "Divine Wind" 57

Chapter 10

The Last Island – Okinawa 63

Chapter 11

Going Home 104

Chapter 12

The Return to Civilian Life 110

Chapter 13

My Own Shop 116

Chapter 14

My Paintings 118

Chapter 15

Post - WW II Echoes of the Red Devil Squadron, VMTB - 232 121

Photographs & Illustrations 130
Letter of Thanks from President Harry S. Truman 143
Commendations to VSB-232 and VMTB-232 and Scoreboard 145
Military Awards to Frank Renda 149
Certificates of Separation and Honorable Discharge 153
Certificates for Post WW-II GI Bill Education 154

Maps of the Pacific Theater: Locations of VMTB-232

The Pacific Areas, Troopship Routes 3
Ulithi Atoll, Falalop Island 48
Okinawa Shima 64
List of VMTB-232 Pacific Voyages and Landfalls 129

Introduction

In 1998, Tom Brokaw aroused the nation's interest in my generation with his book, "The Greatest Generation". His point was that growing up during the deprivations of the Great Depression had developed a tough, resilient, and "can-do" attitude among the Nation's youth. This attitude strengthened them -- and enabled them to fight and win World War II. And, this attitude carried forward after World War II and helped them make America a superpower.

I came to appreciate that I was one of the millions of men who experienced both of these major events in our history during my formative years. My memories of those years remain vivid. I have now told my story – in hopes that today's youth might know what I experienced personally during the Great Depression and World War II.

The Japanese surprise attack on Pearl Harbor on December 7, 1941 shocked the nation. Many Americans rushed to enlist in the military services. Everyone soon had relatives and friends in the armed forces.

I graduated from William Penn High School in York, Pennsylvania in 1943 and enlisted in the U.S. Marine Corps. By this time the country was fully involved in World War II in both the European and Pacific Theaters. The Marine Air Corps trained me to be an armorer for the Grumman Avenger torpedo bomber – a tough and versatile aircraft.

I was assigned to VMTB-232, the Red Devil Marine Air Squadron. It was the most decorated flying squadron in the Marine Air Corps, and I was proud to be in it. VMTB-232 was assigned to the Pacific Theater. They helped to halt the advance of the Japanese at Guadalcanal – and prevented Australia from being cut off from the lifelines from the USA. They then took the offensive to Japan through the islands of the Pacific -- ending with the battle of Okinawa, the largest, longest, highest casualty battle of the War. It was to be the last battle of World War II.

I fought in the battle for Okinawa. It lasted for 82 days – and included massed Kamikaze suicide air attacks that were costly to American forces – especially the Navy. The Japanese were clever and desperate. Their dedication to dying for their Emperor was frightening.

But Pearl Harbor gave a bunch of 18 and 19 year old American kids the strength and courage that only a freedom-loving culture can provide. We endured – and we prevailed. Then, those of us who survived came home to build lives that moved the country forward. We went to school, we went to work, and we raised families. And, we taught our families the lessons that we learned from having lived through the Great Depression and World War II.

I sometimes reflect on today's scene in America with deep concern. I hope that current and future generations will carry on -- and prepare themselves to deal with both the good times and the bad. It will help them to endure to serve America -- and to keep her free and strong.

Frank Renda

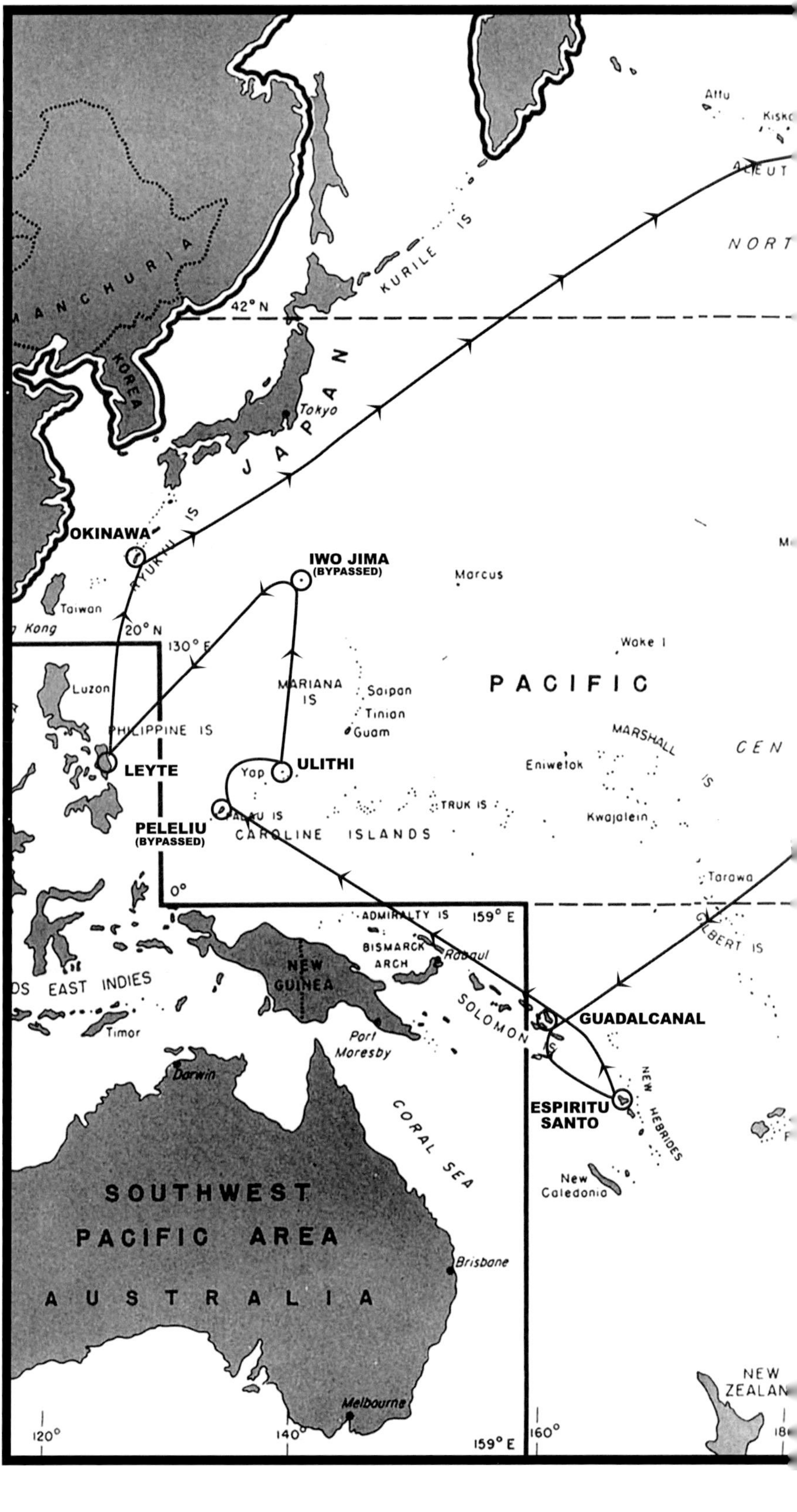

MANCHURIA
KOREA
JAPAN
KURILE IS
Attu
42° N
Tokyo
OKINAWA
RYUKYU IS
IWO JIMA
(BYPASSED)
Marcus
Taiwan
20° N
130° E
Wake I
Luzon
MARIANA IS
Saipan
Tinian
Guam
PACIFIC
PHILIPPINE IS
LEYTE
ULITHI
Yap
MARSHALL IS
Eniwetok
PELELIU
(BYPASSED)
PALAU IS
TRUK IS
Kwajalein
CAROLINE ISLANDS
0°
Tarawa
ADMIRALTY IS
159° E
BISMARCK ARCH
Rabaul
GILBERT IS
EAST INDIES
NEW GUINEA
SOLOMON
GUADALCANAL
Timor
Port Moresby
Darwin
NEW HEBRIDES
ESPIRITU SANTO
CORAL SEA
New Caledonia
SOUTHWEST PACIFIC AREA
AUSTRALIA
Brisbane
Melbourne
NEW ZEALAN
120°
140°
159° E
160°

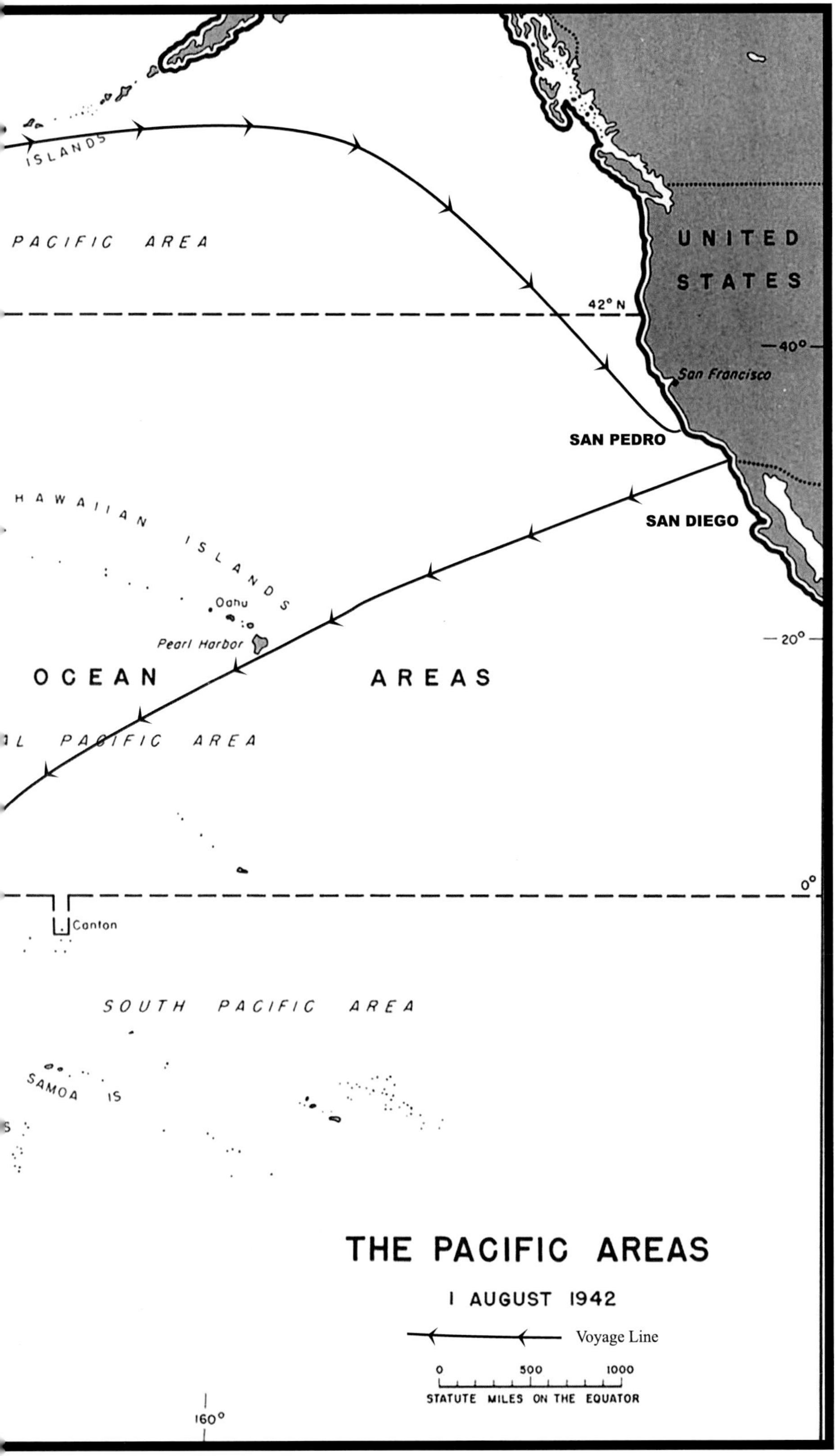

ISLANDS
PACIFIC AREA
UNITED STATES
42° N
40°
San Francisco
SAN PEDRO
SAN DIEGO
HAWAIIAN ISLANDS
Oahu
Pearl Harbor
20°
OCEAN AREAS
PACIFIC AREA
0°
Canton
SOUTH PACIFIC AREA
SAMOA IS
THE PACIFIC AREAS
1 AUGUST 1942
Voyage Line
0 500 1000
STATUTE MILES ON THE EQUATOR
160°

Chapter 1

Early Days

I was born on my Uncle Tony's farm in Lenola, New Jersey on August 4, 1925 to Joseph and Mary Renda. In those days, the doctor and a nurse would come to the house to deliver the baby. When I was delivered, the nurse held me up and said to my mother, "It's a boy!" They told me years later that I then celebrated my arrival by urinating all over the Nurse's chest. In imagining the scene today, I'm very glad that she didn't drop me.

Soon after I was born, I developed pneumonia and a very high fever. The doctor said that I wouldn't last past midnight. But, I somehow managed to hang on. My father said that during the night I kept ripping my lips open with my fingernails. They bled all during the night. This must have brought my fever down, and I lived to tell this story of a Great Depression boyhood and an adventure-filled service in the Pacific with the U. S. Marine Corps during World War II.

My Uncle Tony was my father's older brother -- and the first-born son in a family from the small Sicilian town of Cattolica Eraclea. The Sicilian custom was that the first-born son would be sent to school to be educated. He would be responsible to advise his younger brothers and sisters about worldly things as they worked on the family farm or in the family business. Because of this old-world custom, my father was not educated, and he was to be illiterate for his entire life. He was smart and good with his hands – and was a very kind and generous man. But, this lack of a childhood education was to haunt him. It forever limited his chances for decent-paying employment in America.

Uncle Tony was the first in the family to come to America. He settled on a small farm in Lenola, located about 8 miles east of Camden. My father and mother came from Cattolica Eraclea later, but they were not married at the time. My father settled on the farm with Tony, and my mother went with her family to York, Pennsylvania. Later, they were to meet and marry in York. They were probably introduced through letters that were sent from one Sicilian family to relatives and friends in other Sicilian settlements in America. These letters often included descriptions of young people of marriageable age.

My father immigrated to America on the same voyage as his best friend, Sam Terroso. They stayed at my Uncle's Tony's farm and began to look for work. There were local postings for coal mining jobs that were available in Avella, Pennsylvania – on the border with West Virginia. So, they took the train from Camden to Avella. When they arrived, they rented a room on the second floor of a rooming house in Avella. They were weary from the trip, put their luggage on the bed, and flopped on top of it to take a nap. A few minutes later, a bomb went off somewhere downstairs. Luckily, they rode the bed down to the basement. This was their welcome to the labor violence that existed in the coal mining areas of the Appalachians in the 1920's. They immediately got out of there and took a train back to Camden.

The employment picture picked up shortly after the Avella misadventure. Both my father and Uncle Tony got jobs at the RCA works in Camden. My dad married my mother, who was still living with her family in York, Pennsylvania. They settled with my Uncle Tony on the farm in Lenola. And that's where I was born.

Later, there was a cutback at RCA, and it was rough going from then on. So, our families began to make Italian sausage in the kitchen of the farmhouse in an effort to make a living. Every night, my Uncle Tony's family, my dad and mother and my sister Josephine and I would get together, and we'd make sausage. I remember that they bought pork shoulder at 15 cents a pound and ground it with a hand grinder. They added paprika to the meat. It was an odorless and tasteless sweet red pepper. The paprika gave the ground pork a red color and made it look fresh.

My father had a novel way of cooking his breakfast sausage. He would take 4 or 5 pieces of newspaper and roll the sausage in them. He would twist the ends to keep the roll taut, then stick a fork through the paper and sausage. He would open the door on the pot-bellied stove in the kitchen, and stick the sausage in. The paper would catch fire, and, after it had burned away, the sausage was cooked and ready to eat. It was a simple way to broil the sausage without having to use (and clean) a frying pan.

My father would peddle the sausage door-to-door in Lenola. It was good – and it sold. One day my father knocked at a house, and a man and his wife and their two small children answered the door. My father asked if they would like to buy some sausage. The man said they would love to buy some, but they didn't have any money. When my father saw their situation, he gave them three pounds. I never knew how that went over with my uncle Tony, but that was the kind of man my father was. He was kind-hearted and went out of his way to help people.

My Uncle Tony wasn't the nicest person to live with. He was very stern – I never saw him smile. In fact, I didn't know if he had any teeth. Our family lived with his family in his farmhouse in Lenola, but we weren't allowed in the living room. We had to stay in the kitchen. That was our territory – together with the grounds outside. He had a floor-model radio in the living room. Because we weren't allowed in, we used to lay on the floor in the kitchen to listen to the serial drama "Buck Rogers in the 25th Century" coming through the crack under the closed door. On rare occasions, he would relent and allow us in the living room.

Uncle Tony continued to act towards my father in the Sicilian way – commanding and demanding. He was educated, and my father was not – except for the ability to sign his name. He presumed that he could continue to control my father's life in America – always telling him what to do. Uncle Tony had given my father the money to buy a used car to deliver sausage to outlying neighborhoods. But, he never let my father forget the fact that he had given him the money. One time, he had asked my father to trade cars with him. In one final embarrassment for my father, he had to ask one of his friends to take the New Jersey driver's test for him – because he could not read the traffic signs on the written part of the test. But he drove until he was an old man – and never had an accident.

Unable to read or write, my father also had to rely on Uncle Tony to write to their parents in Sicily to let them know how we were doing. Whenever my father was working, he would give his brother some money to include with the letter. It was common practice among immigrants to send money home to relatives in the "Old Country". Times were always hard in Sicily.

We left the farm and moved to Camden to see if my father could find some work there. In a stroke of luck, Campbell's Soup was hiring at one of their canning factories. Both my father and my mother got jobs in one of their canneries. They rented an apartment on the top floor of a three story house in an Italian neighborhood owned by a man named Beddia.

With both my father and mother working, my sister Josephine and I were put in a small day care center in the neighborhood while they were at work. Josephine was two years older than I was, and I was still in diapers. Every morning on their way to work, my parents would take us to the day care center. We would stop on the way at a little grocery store named Santoni's. They would always get me a banana and my sister an orange -- to ease the separation from our parents for the day.

I remember some of our experiences there. They would put us down for a nap after lunch, but we would climb out of our cribs and play on the floor. One day, I slipped on climbing out of my crib. I fell to the floor and cut my head. When my father arrived to pick me up, he was angry with the staff for not having kept me safe. But, I was at fault. This was an early example of the "spirit of adventure" that I was to have for my entire life. I guess it was a hint of bigger things to come.

Although I was still in diapers, I remembered many things that happened at the day care center. My mother said I couldn't possibly remember those days – because I was so young at the time. As one example, I told her in later years that the rubber sheets on the cribs were black – not white. She said that was so, but she was amazed that I could remember details from when I was so very young. I also remember that they served the afternoon milk in an aluminum cup. The milk appeared to have a pale blue ring where it touched the side of the cup. We never drank milk from anything but a glass at home, and that blue ring made me think that the milk was spoiled. I didn't drink it, and neither did my sister. I remembered that because of the unfamiliar blue color.

At Christmas time, the nursery school had us gather into a big room in the basement. They gave each of us a toy. They also gave us a lollipop shaped like a rooster. They were different colors and flavors. The yellow ones were lemon, and the red ones were cherry.

In another example of childhood memory, I remember we were visiting Mrs. Beddia on the first floor. She sang a bawdy Italian song, and my mother asked her not to sing it in front of me. Mrs. Beddia said, "Oh, what does he know, he's too young to understand." Years later, I upset my mother by singing it to her word for word.

Then, employment began to slack off at Campbell's Soup. My mother cut meat for the soups, but was let go because she wouldn't cut the meat into cubes small enough to suit the boss. I guess homemade cooking for one's family doesn't work in the world of making food for mass consumption.

Later, my father lost his job there because of a general cutback. There were strikes at the plant. I remember going to a union meeting with my mother. The union was probably the Farm Workers of America. As the laid-off workers marched around the plant, they sang songs that ridiculed the plant managers. These were the 1920s, and there were very few production worker unions at the time.

One thing that kept us going during these hard times were the family get-togethers at Zia (Aunt) Rosa's three story house in Camden. Zia Rosa was the mother of my father's best friend Sam Terroso. Zia's daughter Anna was the wife of my Uncle Tony. Zia's children were Sam, Anna, and five other daughters. Zia

Rosa enjoyed having the family – including all her children and their spouses and her grandchildren -- over for Sunday dinner. Her house had a long, connected living room and dining area. And, she had a player piano with some music rolls. After dinner, she would start the player piano, and all the little kids would jump around and dance. The adults would remain at the dinner table, have a glass of wine, and talk. I always remember these gatherings as some of the best times I had as a kid.

There were some other events that happened at these gatherings. One time, someone said, "I smell gas!" I followed Zia Rosa's husband Nino into the kitchen as he went to search for a gas leak. He lit a match and ran it up and down the gas pipe to the stove. At one point, a flame shot out about 8 inches. He said, "Wait a minute, I'll be right back." He went down to the basement and came back with a wrench. He began to tighten the connection in the gas pipe, and the flame gradually went out. I often think back and wonder if the house could have blown up.

Another time, I was out in the yard with their dog. The dog began to foam at the mouth. Nino saw this and ran into the house. He came back with a pistol. The dog was running around in the yard, and Nino was shooting at it. After several shots, he killed it. What surprised me was how people could shoot in their yard – and no cops showed up to see what the shooting was about. In fact, I never saw a cop during the years we lived in the Camden area.

Depression days continued to hold us in the grip of poverty. To recover from the loss of his job at Campbell's Soup, my father and four of his unemployed friends tried to think of some way to make money. They learned that women were not buying ready-to-wear dresses for either themselves or their daughters – probably because they were uncertain as to how long the hard times would last. So, my father and his four friends thought – why not buy bolts of dress materials, and sell "just enough" cloth to make a dress off the bolt while going door-to-door?

As risky as this scheme sounds, it worked. They must have hit a sweet spot in women's perceived need to save money by sewing for themselves and their daughters. The five peddlers knocked on doors in Camden – and found eager buyers. At the end of the season, each of the lucky five celebrated their success by buying a new 1929 Ford Model "A" sedan. And, their earnings allowed them to pay with cash! All the cars were all black, but they each chose different color wheels – black, yellow, white, green and red. Colored wheels were a model variation of the times.

I was fascinated by the little glass cup in the gas line under the hood of my father's Model A. The water that was in the gas would separate and collect in the bottom of the cup. (At that time, most gas stations had leaky underground storage tanks that would allow water to leak into the gas.) Every week or so, my father would remove the cup and drain out the water.

The following summer, we'd load up the Model A with a basket of food and drive to Atlantic City. We'd sit under the boardwalk and have our noonday lunch. The only problem was that sand would fall down through the cracks in the boards. So, you had to find a spot where the people weren't walking. That became our ritual Sunday outing in the summertime.

On the way home from one of these Sundays at the beach, I remember that we stopped at an airport along the road. I was just a little guy – about four years old. We had pulled over alongside a wire fence where people had gathered to watch the planes take off and land. From a distance, they looked so small, and I thought they were toys. So, I tried to crawl under the fence. My father grabbed me by the seat of my pants and said, "What are you doing?" I said, "I want to get one of those planes." Some people who were gathered at the fence laughed at my mistake.

But, nobody standing there could have known that in a few short years I would get my hands on all the full-sized planes I could handle: I would have the responsibility to arm U.S. Marine combat aircraft on islands in the faraway western Pacific.

Hard times came again to Camden, and we moved to York where my mother's family still lived. My father tried to find work there, but things were slow. There were some now-and-then menial jobs – but nothing permanent.

And, that's where I first went to school. I was in the first grade at St. Patrick's school in York. One thing I remember is that all the nuns called me Francis – and tried to get me to use Francis as my name. But, I kept telling them, "My name is Frank." I guess the difference mattered to me even then.

Then we moved back to the farm in Lenola. My father wanted to look for work there. This time we did not live in Uncle Tony's house. There was another, smaller house on the farm, and we moved into it. The back yards of the two houses met in an L-shape. I went to second grade in a farm area school in Lenola.

My Uncle Tony had a dog named King. He would always come over to our place and stay with me. He was with me constantly, and gradually he became "my" dog. I'd hook him to a little wagon, and he'd pull me around the farm. Uncle Tony would call him with, "Here King, here King". But I'd say, "Stay here King" – and the dog wouldn't move. He would listen to me instead of anyone else. I always wanted a pet, and we formed a true bond.

In the summer, my Sister Josephine and I had the job of going to an ice house to get a block of ice for the ice box. The icehouse was about a block away from the farm. And we'd take turns pushing and pulling the wagon. For refreshment, we'd lick the ice block on the way home. And I still remember kids telling us to scoop up tar along the road when it would get soft from the summer sun. And, as the story went, if you chewed the tar, your teeth would get white. So we scooped it up with a stick and chewed. Looking back, I don't think that was very sanitary.

My father's friend-for-life Sam Terroso and his wife Anna would occasionally visit us at the farm. Times were hard, and they would bring me clothes – trousers and shirts. They would buy the trousers long, and I would have to roll them up. But, I grew into them and they were OK.

Then, we left the farm and moved back to Camden. We piled our furniture on an old truck and started down the road. I can still see King chasing the truck. He ran for about a mile – and finally dropped from exhaustion. It was a sad moment for me.

In Camden, we moved into a second story apartment on Stevens street in the "Little Italy" section. The rent was cheaper because it was smaller than the third floor apartment we had lived in before.

I went to third grade. What I remember most was a very nice teacher named Miss Kline. One day she brought a pint bottle of cream, an empty quart milk bottle, and some crackers. She poured the cream into the quart bottle and had each student shake the bottle ten times. By the time it got around the entire class of forty students, there was butter in the bottle. Then she gave each student a dab of butter on a cracker so that we could taste the butter we had just made. She used this simple demonstration that involved the entire class, but I never forgot it.

While I was in third grade, my father repeatedly asked me to teach him how to read and write in English. He thought -- that because I was learning -- I could teach him. I tried and tried, but it just didn't work. He had never learned to read and write in Italian – so he had no previous knowledge of reading and writing a language. And, I was too young to understand how to teach him. It was a sad experience for both of us

There was a park near Camden named Cooper Park. It had a swimming pool for kids, and the people from Camden would pile in and fill it up. They didn't have a water filtering system, and the water was dirty brown. We went there once, but my father never took us back. I remember coming home after we were there, and my father stopped at a barber shop. He had the barber cut off all my sister's hair. There was a Sicilian folk belief that – if you had all your hair cut off – it would grow back stronger. (Maybe the dirty water in the pool had caused him to get her hair cut just then.)

With her hair suddenly gone, my sister started to cry. So we stopped along the way home at a store and my father bought each of us an ice cream cone. That settled her down a bit.

I remember going to the barber shop with him another time. He got a haircut, and then I got a haircut. When I was done, I started to cry. He said, "Why are you crying?" I said, "He cut my sideburns off!" I wanted my haircut to be just like my father's. Maybe I was interested in being a barber from an early age – but I don't really know.

The depression continued, and everyone was short of money. Men would go door-to-door to buy gold from people. I remember that my mother sold her wedding band for two dollars. She dropped it into a milk bottle they used to collect the gold items they bought.

I also remember that I had two toys. One was a little bicycle that you wound up and it would go around in a circle – and a bell would ring. The other toy was a little wooden canoe that someone gave to me when we lived at the farm. To keep the other kids from getting my toys, I hid them in the cabinet of my mother's sewing machine.

I came home from school one day, and the sewing machine was gone! I asked my mother where it was, and she said she sold it. And my toys were in there! The depression had many victims. Some were bankers and brokers who lost fortunes, and at least one was a small boy who lost his only toys.

There was a bakery about three doors down the street. If you made your own pizza, they'd bake it in their oven for ten cents. My mother would do that sometimes as one way to feed us a hot meal.

Once in a while, we were allowed to go to a movie – when the tickets were only ten cents. On the way, there were signs of the times. There was a black man who sat alongside the sidewalk and played a guitar. He had his hat on the ground at his feet, and people passing by would drop some coins into it.

And there was a guy who had built a tree house, and he sat up in it for days at a time. He had a bucket on a rope, and people would send food and water up to him. And people would give him money to help him feed his family.

At the movie, they would take your ticket and draw the stubs. The winner got a new bicycle. But, I never saw anyone walk away with one. Today, I wonder if the theater owner "recycled" it to a friend or relative. Was this a scheme to increase movie attendance? But, who knows: People were desperate.

My Father got a pushcart and worked the streets of Camden. He sold hot dogs, root beer, and pie. My sister and I would wait behind the curtain at the window of our apartment and look for him to come home at night. We could see him park his pushcart in the alley across the street. We hoped that he would have something left for us to eat. And, he always did – some pie, a hot dog, and some root beer. And that's what we looked forward to every night for supper.

Another thing I remembered from the scenes on Stevens Street was that there were hardly any cars around. People would walk in the streets until they were crowded. It was like walking through the aisles at a county fair.

And I remember there was a bench in front of this one house, and there sat Sicilians from all parts of Sicily and southern Italy. I would stand there and listen to them talking in the many regional dialects they spoke. They fascinated me. I would stand there for hours listening to them. I picked up a lot of words – including one that was similar in several dialects. It sounded like "endugway" – which means "and so on and so forth".

I didn't know it at the time, but one day I would make good use of my knowledge of languages.

CHAPTER 2

GROWING UP IN YORK, PENNSYLVANIA

A few words about the origins of the York community may be helpful to understanding how a small colony of newly-immigrated Sicilian families struggled to settle into an area populated by a large, long-established and nearly homogeneous majority of Pennsylvania Germans. The two groups differed as to ethnic and religious backgrounds – and to the historical time of immigration.

The City of York was established in 1741. The city, and the surrounding York County area, was settled mostly by Pennsylvania Germans (more popularly known as the Pennsylvania Dutch) in the mid 1700's – together with a relatively few Scotch-Irish. York had a significant colonial history. In 1777-78 the Continental Congress met in York to write and adopt the Articles of Confederation for the newly independent colonies. These were the first documents to use the term, "The United States of America". Because of this, York claims to be the "Birthplace of the Nation", and the "First Capital of the United States". Yorkers are proud of their having served this key role in the founding of the nation – just prior to the Declaration of Independence.

York and the surrounding county enjoyed the continuous growth of many successful industries and farms. Because of its early settlement and subsequent population growth, workers were available locally to serve the rapid growth of industries in the late nineteenth century. There was no need for local industries to encourage late nineteenth or early twentieth century mass immigrations from different countries in Europe -- as was the case for most Pennsylvania cities.

By the early twentieth century, the Pennsylvania Dutch majority had a population that had lived in York County for ten generations or more. They were closely knit, and justly proud both of who they were – and of their accomplishments throughout the history of Colonial America and of the United States. They built industries that became known for quality products the world over. They fought in every war – beginning with the American Revolution. For any new immigrant group that was different in both ethnic and religious backgrounds, entering the York community presented challenges to both their assimilation and acceptance. The Sicilian community would work hard at both, and it would be a long and gradual process. The "New Kids" on the block would have to overcome the powerful "show me" demands of the established community. Basic human nature was at work here.

In 1934, we moved to York from the "Little Italy" section of Camden, New Jersey. Fortunately, there was also a "Little Italy" section in York -- just southwest of the city square. We settled there to get our start in the community. It was helpful that the small Italian community that existed in York was also from Cattolica Eraclea – the Sicilian hometown of my father and mother. My mother's family had been living in York from when they first immigrated to America. And, my father and mother knew many of the families and friends from the "Old Country".

A number of my father's friends from Cattolica Eraclea were educated and had done well. They bought houses on West Princess Street and in the surrounding neighborhood. They lived in some of the houses -- and rented others mostly to people in the Sicilian immigrant community. My father always rented apartments from people he knew from Sicily. He believed that Sicilians looked out for each other, and he thought that they gave him a break on the rent. The houses that faced the alleys had lower rents than the houses that faced the streets. He rented our first apartment on Cherry Alley.

Times were hard, and there was very little steady work available. Growing up in depression days, we would have spaghetti every night. It provided a low-cost meal that would fill you. My father would buy spaghetti by the case to get it for the lowest cost possible. My mother didn't have money to put meat in the sauce, so she would bring the sauce to a boil and break an egg or two in there – and the eggs would cook in the sauce. This made a tasty supper.

Our Cherry Alley apartment had a coin-operated gas meter in the basement. When my mother was cooking and the burner flame began to fade, she'd give me a quarter and tell me to hurry down to the basement and feed the meter. I would run down and put the quarter in and turn the lever, and then the flame would come back. If you didn't feed the meter, it would automatically cut off the gas. We also had a pot belly stove in the living room. It had a hot air pipe that went up to the second floor. But, we shut off the baffle because the heat went up there anyway through the stair well. Just below the baffle was a hot air discharge grille. Every morning, I would put a slice of bread on each side of the grille, and that's how I made toast for my breakfast.

Early each morning we would get a quart of milk from a milkman. In the winter the aluminum cap would freeze the cream, and it would be pushed up and out of the bottle about an inch. Before anyone would take in the milk, I'd take a knife and cut the raised cream off. Then I'd put the lid back on. It was like eating ice cream. I didn't tell anyone because I didn't want to get into trouble for cream theft.

My father found work with the Works Progress Administration, a Federal Government program established to put people to work during the depression. One WPA project was to install stabilizing stone along the banks of the Codorus Creek where it ran through York. This project was part of a nation- wide government effort to provide flood control -- and to prevent erosion of riverbanks throughout the country. Like most WPA projects, it came to an end after a year or so.

When the Codorus erosion control project was completed, my father got a job in the iron foundry of the York Manufacturing Co. A number of men from "Little Italy" worked at this iron foundry. It was hot and dirty work. They would walk to work every morning across the College Avenue Bridge. Some of the Negroes who lived in that area would throw rocks at the men as they were walking home to "Little Italy". I guess that people from the black community had traditionally held most of these foundry jobs. They were probably displaced by desperate new immigrants who would work bottom end jobs for less.

One day, one of the guys from "Little Italy" brought a pistol. When the rocks began to fly on the way home, he shot a couple of rounds into the air. Luckily, nobody was hit. There were no cops in the area, and that was the end of the rock throwing.

Whenever he was working, my father would resume sending money to his parents in Sicily. Uncle Tony was still at the farm in Lenola. But my mother could read and write. She now wrote the letters and included the money – saying that it was from their son, Joseph. My father's parents wrote back to my mother and asked why he had never sent money before.

This is how my father learned that Uncle Tony was sending the money he had been giving him – but never said it was from my father! The parents presumed the money was from my Uncle Tony. After this discovery, my father and his brother were forever "on the outs" (estranged). This event really upset me too. It was so like my uncle to have done this. Like my father, I never forgot it – nor forgave him for it.

I entered the fourth grade at the Central Elementary School in downtown York. I got off to an awkward start. The school system dentist and his assistant came in every so often to check the students' teeth. At my first exam, the dentist said,

"Do you have a toothbrush?" I said, "Yeah, we have a toothbrush. We all use the same one." We didn't own a toothbrush, but I thought I'd say something to him so he wouldn't think there wasn't a toothbrush in the family. Then he looked at his assistant -- and they smiled at each other. He could tell I wasn't brushing my teeth. But, we didn't own a toothbrush because we were so poor.

I was involved in another strange event in the fourth grade. One day, the kid sitting behind me touched my shoulder. I instinctively began to turn my head. Just then, Miss Ruler (not her real name) yelled, "Get up here!" I went to the front of the classroom, and she put me over the front desk. Then she whaled the daylights out of me with a 2 inch-wide yardstick. I had made up my mind that I wasn't going to cry – and I didn't. I still remember the faces of all the students looking at me. Their mouths were open, and their eyes were real big. They were shocked in disbelief. Then Miss Ruler stopped and said, "Let that be a lesson to you." But, I hadn't done anything to deserve that hard a punishment. I can still see those faces. Later, I began to wonder if there was something about me that irritated her and caused her to hit me so hard.

In the fifth grade of Central Elementary, I had a teacher named Miss Sechrist. One day, she was teaching the lesson, but I wasn't paying attention. I often sketched things or people when I was bored in class. On this day, I was sketching her. The next thing I know, she's standing beside me. And I thought, boy, am I in trouble now. She looked down at the sketch and said, "May I have this?" She didn't sound angry. I said yes – and gave her the sketch. I wasn't called to the principal's office, confronted with the sketch and lectured for inattention. I think she liked it and kept it. I had enjoyed sketching from an early age – it just came naturally to me. And I still like to paint and draw. I've been doing it all my life.

In the sixth grade, one of my teachers was a sister of "Miss Ruler" from fourth grade. I wondered if she was going to use a ruler on me too. But, she was very nice – and nothing like her sister. She taught music. She had every student sing in front of the class. When it was my turn, I sang, and she said, "You have to take up music." I didn't know whether she liked my voice or the way I sang – or whatever it was. But I thought, yeah, that'll be the day. We weren't sure that we could afford our next meal, and she's telling me I should go to music school.

After Central Elementary, I went to Hannah Penn Junior High School. They taught art in seventh, eight, and ninth grades. All of my art teachers liked my work and said the same thing: "You have to go to art school." But it was the same story. We didn't have the money for me to go to any special school.

About this time, I began to run everywhere I went. One time, a neighbor stopped me on the street and said, "Hey kid, don't you ever walk?" But, running became my natural pace. If I went to the store, I ran. Somehow, I just had the energy to do it.

While at Hannah Penn, I was on the track team. I was a pretty good runner and high jumper. But, I was the only kid on the team that they didn't give track shoes. I had to wear my own shoes. I was never quite sure what that meant.

The summer after I graduated from Hannah Penn, I asked my father if I could stay out later than my usual 9 p.m. curfew. He said, "No, I want you in by 9 p.m." I asked him why. He said," I'll tell you why. The last feature at the movies has started, and all the stores are closed. There's nothing out there but trouble, and I want you home" He went on to say, "I know you're a good kid. You never get into trouble. But when you're with a group of boys, and they get into trouble, you're an accomplice – and you're going to be in trouble also. So you get home". I didn't have an answer for him. When I thought about it later, I knew he was right. That was a pretty good piece of advice on how a kid should be raised. And I always respected his wishes – because I knew what he expected of me.

After Hannah Penn, I went to William Penn Senior High for grades 10 through 12. I was interested in becoming a machinist. So, I signed up for a dual program where I took classes in History, English and Spanish in the morning -- and Machine Shop in the afternoon. The Machine Shop classes were taught in the Atreus Wanner building. It was separate from, but close to, the high school. York had many manufacturing plants, and they provided a steady demand for young people who were trained in machine shop practices, and who had hands-on training in operating machines.

When I was at William Penn, all the boys had to take gym for an hour every day. The school had abandoned team sports during regular gym classes. Instead, they had us do push-ups and all kinds of exercises -- to prepare us for military service. They then had us run up and down the bleachers in the gym. All of this physical activity got us into really good shape.

About this time, I started to get whiskers. I shaved with my father's straight razor. One day I got a splinter under my toenail. So, I used his straight razor to cut away the toenail to get the splinter out. When my father next went to shave, he said, "What happened to my razor?" I told him what happened, but he didn't get angry about it. I thought it would upset him, but for some reason it didn't. Maybe he thought it was good thinking on my part.

I also had a couple of temporary jobs in tenth grade. I worked at the Sanitary Barber Shop on East Philadelphia Street as a shoeshine boy. And, thanks to my experience with a straight razor, I could already give a decent shave. Sometimes, when some customer would want a shave in a hurry, the barber would say, "Frank, get him on the back chair and shave him." The customers may have wondered whether they could trust me or not, but I did all right with it. The barber charged the customer, but I never got anything out of it. I don't remember what the excuse was for not paying me. I guess the tough times were supposed to make you glad for learning opportunities. It was just plain unfair to me.

In 1941, I got a temporary job at Western Union – delivering telegrams as a bicycle messenger. On December seventh, I was waiting for the next delivery, and I saw the telegraph operator turn white as he watched a message coming in. He tore the tape off the ticker and pasted it on a telegram form. He sealed it, and told me to take it to City Hall – and to not show it to anyone.

So, I rode to City Hall -- which was on Duke Street at the time. It was right across from the Yorktowne Hotel on the corner of an alley in an old brick building. I walked in and there was a counter with two policemen, one standing on either side. One policeman said, "What do you want?" I said, "I was told to deliver this telegram here". And they said, "Who's it for?" I said, "I don't know, they just told me to deliver it here."

The policeman behind the counter opened it and began to read it out loud. "The United States is in a state of war. Pearl Harbor has been bombed." He looked at me and said, "Where in the hell is Pearl Harbor?" I said I didn't know. The other policeman didn't know either. So, just by chance, I carried the message to the York City Hall that announced the beginning of America's entry into World War II.

Almost immediately, the government called for the collection of scrap aluminum to make airplanes. The city erected a wire enclosure on the southeast corner of the York square to collect scrap aluminum for the war effort. People would put old aluminum pots and pans into this enclosure. Some people actually bought new pots and pans and put them in with the price tags still on. We were at war, and people wanted to do their part for the war effort.

Local manufacturers had devised the "York Plan" to deal with the demands of war production. The York Plan surveyed every shop – large and small – to see if they could provide machines to make parts for war effort contracts. It made maximum use of each factory and small shop in York. The plan was very successful and became nationally known and copied.

I worked in the machine shop at the Goodling Electric Company on Springdale Avenue after school – making brass bushings for 40 mm anti-aircraft guns. My sister Josephine had also gone to the machine shop program at William Penn. She was already working there – making pistons for the same 40 mm guns.

In the eleventh grade, my father urged me to "Learn a trade." So, I signed up as an apprentice for barber training. The barber was related to our family. He would take an apprentice and train him for two years. He told me that the rules of the apprentice program were that I would have to work for the entire two years without pay. He said that if I worked for him, he would feed me. So, after school was out – evenings, weekends, and vacations -- I would go to his shop to learn barbering.

Between the machine shop course and the barber apprenticeship, I was learning two trades at the same time at the age of sixteen. I went to the barber shop after school and worked until 10 p.m. During summer vacations, I worked from 8 a.m. until 10 p.m.

I got so good at barbering that the barber would go hunting for a week or two and leave me to run the shop. When he'd come home he'd say, "If you want something to eat, there's groundhog on the dining room table." That was his idea of feeding me! But I wouldn't eat groundhog. Instead, I'd go next door to a little grocery and buy a pie for a nickel. That's what I survived on until I got home -- where my mother always had some leftover food for me.

One week when the barber was away hunting, I took in $44. This was when haircuts were 25 cents for adults and 15 cents for kids. When he returned, I was proud to tell him how much I had made for the shop. And he said, "I'm not allowed to pay you anything." I wasn't sure what the apprentice program rules were, but I had worked all week and didn't think there was a clause that said he couldn't pay me – even under the circumstances of my running the shop without his supervision. I still think he could have given me something. This just didn't seem fair to me. So, I picked up my tools and left.

I had put in the better part of two years and had almost finished the practical part of my apprenticeship. But, I didn't take the barber license test. There was a war on, and I knew I was going to enlist into the service rather than wait to be drafted. And, there was always the chance that I wouldn't come back. So, I decided to wait until after I got back from the service to take my test.

My Uncle Tony had moved to York in about 1942 or 1943 because his son Frank had opened a beauty shop on South George Street the year before. Uncle Tony knew people in York who had also come from Cattolica Eraclea. One day I saw him on the street with Tony Torterricci, a friend of his who also knew me. Tony Torterricci recognized me and said to my uncle, "Do you know this young man?" His intention was to reintroduce Uncle Tony and me after years of being "on the outs". But, my uncle replied to him in Italian, "Who knows him." This is a Sicilian insult that meant that I was not worth knowing. Uncle Tony didn't know that I now both understood and spoke Italian.

So, with the memories of his taking credit for the money that my father had sent to their parents still in my mind, I bristled and said to him, "You don't know me - and I don't know you." I said this in Italian, and my uncle reacted to this counter insult with an explosion. He yelled, "I'll bust your ass -- and your father's ass". Tony Torterricci didn't want us to get involved in an altercation on the street, and he appealed to my uncle to calm down. My uncle would have none of it, so I turned and walked away.

They were beginning to draft people. When I turned 18, I told my father that I wanted to enlist. He said, "Why don't you wait until you are drafted?" I said, "No, I think I want to get into the Navy – in the submarine service."

Tony Ragusa, one of my next-door neighbors on Cherry Alley, had already enlisted in the Marine Corps. He had fought on Guadalcanal in 1942 – where the U.S. forces stopped and turned back the Japanese advance in the Solomon Islands. He had come home on leave, and I was really taken by his appearance. He was wearing the attractive Marine Corps dress blues – with battle ribbons. That did it: I decided to enlist in the Marine Corps.

I began to wonder as to what my life in the Marine Corps might be like. Where in the world would I be sent? What type of action would I see? Would I come home to York – and in one piece?

The realization that my life was about to change drastically caused me to remember many of the little things that I had experienced as a kid growing up in York. My memories were mostly of depression era happenings in the neighborhood where we lived. Even today, I can recall many events that were part of my life. They didn't seem to be that important at the time. But, they were part of my growing up in York, and they have remained in my memory for my whole life.

For example, the garbage wagons in York were horse-drawn, and the horses had tassels on their harnesses to shoo the flies away. When the horses would walk or shiver, the tassels would swing and the flies would fly off. When the wagons would stop, the flies would resettle on the horses. The wagons for the wet garbage were made from metal tanks that would keep any "juice" from leaking onto the pavement. For the dry garbage, they would use regular wagons.

The ice wagon would come every morning, and we would put the card in the window to show the iceman what weight block of ice we wanted that day for the ice box. And, the drain pan under the ice box had to be pulled out and emptied of the water from the melted ice every day. That was my job.

We kids would run after the ice wagon and pick chips of ice from the pavement to suck on. In looking back on this, it was probably risky to our health to have picked ice chips off pavement used by horse-drawn wagons. But, what do you know when you're a kid. The ice chips were a treat. Today, a snow cone vendor comes to a neighborhood in a truck, rings a bell, and kids flock to the truck. (This seems like a big improvement, but I bet we enjoyed our frozen treats as much as they enjoy theirs.)

Speaking of horses, my mother got burned when she dropped a pot of hot coffee on her arm. It turned red. My father went out, got some horse manure, put it on her arm and wrapped it. Years later, I told one of the customers at my barber shop about this – presuming it was some type of foolish Sicilian folk remedy and must have been very unsanitary. The customer was a surgeon, and -- to my surprise -- he said that was the best thing my father could have done under the circumstances. He said that there is a type of acid in the horse manure that will take away the pain. I guess some folk remedies work – even if we don't know why.

In addition to the usual fruit and vegetable vendors who would come to the neighborhood, there were farmers who would come through the alleys and sell rabbits from the beds of their pickup trucks. The rabbits were gutted, and they had stuffed them with grass to keep out the flies. There were stacks of them in the truck, and they cost twenty five cents apiece. We would buy one of these fresh rabbits once in a while, and my mother would cook it in spaghetti sauce. It gave us a tasty and cheap meat dish.

The Fox Bakery in York was near the Valencia Ballroom. You could go there with a pull wagon, and for fifty cents, they would give you a cardboard box filled with bread, pies and cakes. They were day-old baked goods that they brought back from stores when they restocked the shelves with fresh baked goods. We would go there once a week and load up with the day-olds. They were such a treat for us.

I remember when my Father worked at the American Chain Company, he'd bring home pieces of the large leather belts they used to drive the machinery. These belts would wear and break, and they would put the scraps in the trash barrels. These scraps were useful for many things. My father would bring some of these scraps home, borrow an anvil from a neighbor, and resole my shoes. He used carpet tacks to nail on the soles and heels.

But, when I walked down the street, the heads of the tacks would go click, click, click on the sidewalk. Every time someone came along, I'd stop until they had passed by – and then I'd start walking again. I did this until the heads had worn off the tacks – and you didn't hear the clicking anymore. It was just one of those embarrassing things you had to put up with because we couldn't afford a shoemaker.

My father worked at American Chain for about ten years. It was a job, but it was in the "acid room". That's where the chains were washed in hot acid baths to remove the lubricants necessary to bend the chain links in the machinery. The fumes were hazardous, and he began to have trouble breathing. His lungs made him chronically ill for the rest of his life.

My mother worked in a cigar factory for a while. Then she got a job at McKay Chain – measuring bulk chain by weighing it. She worked there for twenty years and retired.

My father later worked as a janitor at Graybill's Electric – a large electrical parts supplier in York. One night as he started his shift, he walked into the manager's office and saw stacks of bills sitting on the desk. Someone had left this money on the desk instead of putting it away. My father got newspapers and covered the money so that it couldn't be seen by someone who might help themselves.

My mother washed clothes on a washboard. Then she got a washing machine. But, the wringer rollers were not electric powered. She had to turn a hand crank to wring the water out of the clothes.

And there was a place in one of the alleys where a guy sold live chickens. You could buy a chicken, take it home, kill it yourself, and pluck the feathers. One day, my mother bought a chicken. She took it down to the basement, held it up by its feet, and stretched its neck to kill it. My mother had very strong hands – and she accidentally pulled the chicken's head off. The chicken began the proverbial running around with its head off, and there was blood flying everywhere. It finally dropped over.

Sadly, I also remembered the anti-Italian feelings in York. Even in school, I could feel it in class. Most of the teachers just looked down on us. They didn't bring us together with the other students. I remembered again that when I was on the track team at Hannah Penn Junior High, they gave track shoes to everyone on the team but me. I ran in a pair of my own shoes.

Looking back, I remember the teachers would go around in class and help the other students. But they never tried to help us with anything. You either got it or you didn't. I began to have the feeling that we were being looked down upon and shunned. We felt it.

It didn't help that our house was within a block of York's red light district on Howard alley. We didn't want to give our address to people – fearing that they would make the connection. We always detoured around the block to avoid seeing the girls hanging out of the windows. If they saw us, they would call to us -- taunting us for their own amusement.

And, at the time, I accepted the anti-Italian feelings as the way things were. We were kids of immigrant parents who were too poor to be well fed, well washed, well dressed, and well spoken.

The only exceptions were the art teachers. When they saw that I had a talent for sketching, they took an interest in me and encouraged me to go to art school. I'll always thank them for that. It gave me enough self-esteem to keep me going.

These are a few of the things I remember about the physical surroundings of my boyhood in York. Although we were poor and our living quarters were old and in the low-rent district, we enjoyed a warm and loving family life. That was the most important part of my boyhood, and it served to carry me through some difficult future times.

Also, depression times required a different way of living. I don't regret those times, because that was the way we had to live to survive. And many other people had to do the same. I think it made us tough and resourceful -- and prepared us for the even darker days that were soon to come.

Chapter 3

The First Island – Boot Camp

I turned eighteen in August of 1943 and registered for the draft. But, I really wanted to enlist in the Marines. My father was still trying to convince me to wait until I was called, but I did not want to wait any longer. So, I took the bus from York to the registration center in Harrisburg with a group of draftees to take my pre-induction physical exam and to enlist in the Marines. After I passed my physical, they were going to put me in the Navy. I said, "No, I wasn't drafted, I'm here to enlist in the Marines". But they didn't register Marine enlistees in Harrisburg. That was done in Philadelphia. So, they put me on a train, but I got there too late to register that day. They gave me a cot for the night at the Philadelphia registration center. I enlisted the next morning. After enlisting, I went home. They had given me 14 days to get my things in order before I had to report for Marine boot camp at Parris Island, South Carolina.

After the 14 days were up, I took a train from York to Parris Island. It was loaded with Marine enlistees from New Jersey, New York, and Pennsylvania. It took a long time to get there, and we had to sleep overnight on the train. There were no sleeping cars, and we spent the night dozing in our seats. We stopped for breakfast somewhere in North Carolina. They served us hominy grits. I didn't know what they were -- so I didn't eat any. We continued to go south, still trying to get some sleep in our seats. We stopped at several stations along the way. At every stop, there were some little colored kids who would dance on the station platform. The guys would toss coins out the railroad car windows to them. Along with the grits, the dancing of those little kids was something else I had never seen before.

We finally arrived at Parris Island. There was no bridge to the island where we got off the train. We had to go to the island on a barge. Once we got on the island, all the young boot campers who had been there for a few weeks looked at us and began to give us the traditional "You'll be sorry" call. They dragged out the word 'sorry' for effect -- and they sounded as though they really meant it. I guessed this first bit of hazing was an introduction to Boot Camp events to come.

As we were walking to our tent area, I saw an older Marine with a beard. He stood out because facial hair was not allowed. I asked a guy who he was, and he said, "That's Lou Diamond." Later, I heard a story of how he had sunk a Japanese ship with a mortar shell – dropping it right down the smokestack.

They later told me that legends about Lou Diamond had circulated so far and so fast that they had become distorted. The facts were that he was a talented Marine Gunnery Sergeant who had developed the new and very effective mortar tactics being used by the Marines in the Pacific. Mortars were important to Marines. Unlike artillery, they were portable and could be hand-carried to firing positions. With the right amount of training, Marines could lay down devastating fire from a bank of mortars, and quickly pick them up and move to different positions.

And, they also told me that Lou Diamond had personally directed mortar fire against Japanese destroyers and cruisers that had taken positions just offshore during the pivotal battle for the island of Guadalcanal in 1942. Japanese ships were trying to align themselves to shell Marine positions onshore. But, Lou's mortar barrages harassed the Japanese crews and they had to keep moving their ships. This upset their plans to deliver organized and accurate fire. It is no exaggeration to say that he disrupted their battle plans and saved Marine casualties from coordinated Japanese naval bombardments. He deserves to be a legend.

And, I knew that my neighbor, Tony Ragusa, was an airplane mechanic who had fought with Marine Air Squadron VMSB – 232 at Henderson Field on Guadalcanal. There is a chance that Lou Diamond's mortar squads had protected Tony from the Japanese naval artillery.

The next thing for us was the official "welcome" to Parris Island. They had us remove all our clothes, and then they quickly cut off all our hair with electric clippers. The guys who had head lice were painted all over their bodies with some kind of blue ointment. This ointment killed the head lice, and these guys were segregated until the ointment had done its work. They had to shower to remove it. (About 1 in 20 of the recruits had head lice.)

Then they fitted us with the uniforms of boot camp -- dungarees and high shoes. They fit shoes by having us stand and hold a fifty pound weight. This weight was less than that of a field pack, but it was enough to make your feet spread. Then they measured your feet for shoes, and the shoes they threw at you really fit.

Then they took us to a barracks as Boot Camp Platoon 751. There, everyone had to learn how to make his cot. The Drill Instructor gave the 72 guys in our platoon a certain amount of time to complete making our cots. If the cots weren't all done to the requirements of appearance and tautness in the allotted amount of time, the DI would call to have all the cots torn down. Next, under his not-so-gentle urging, we would try again. He told the platoon that we were going to repeat the process until everyone could do it in the time allowed. The guys who didn't get it done in time were getting angry looks from those who did – because they had to remake their cots also.

Every morning before breakfast, we had to scrub the floors in our barracks on our hands and knees. The floors were wood, and they were white from the daily scrubbing with water and scrub brushes. We were hardly ever in the barracks, but every morning we had to get water in buckets and scrub the floors.

And, every morning at breakfast, everyone had to eat 4 or 5 prunes. Our bodies soon became accustomed to this regimen. When you had finished breakfast and got back to the barracks, everyone had to run to the latrine and have a bowel movement. They got our bodies adjusted so that everyone was timed to be on the same schedule.

One thing I noticed -- I was eating more food on a regular basis than I had ever eaten before in my life. We had milk at every breakfast, and I began to gain weight – as muscle. Eating sufficient amounts of food regularly was a welcome contrast to the circumstances and habits of my depression-days youth.

We weren't in the barracks all day. They took us to the drill field. They taught us how to march, and to do push-ups and other calisthenics. And every exercise was done for 50 repetitions. If you couldn't do 50 push-ups at first, the DI would get behind you and pull you up by your belt. All other exercises were done at 50 reps also. (The DI would count to 50 out loud.)

If you didn't know how to swim, they'd march you to an area where there were swimming pools. Everyone had to know how to swim. Marines traveled to battle areas by transport ships and landing craft – and often found themselves in the water whether it was planned or not. In the morning, we'd see guys from other platoons marching between the rows of tents on their way to swimming lessons. The ability to swim was a key skill: Your life might depend on it someday.

Everyone was issued a Garand M-1 rifle. You had to learn how to take it apart, clean it, put it back together, and fire it. And that's what you did all morning long – until you could almost do it blindfolded. You had to know your weapon. As the DI's would say, "Your weapon is your friend: Don't ever be without it."

The Marine vocabulary is short, loud, and made up mostly of four-letter words.

The morning command to scrub the floors in the barracks wasn't complete without the DI's saying, "All right, when I give the command – all I want to see is "a__holes and elbows". This traditional urging is common to all branches of the service. It must work. It is usually combined with, "When I say s____, I want you to squat and strain." This was applied not only to the morning scrubbing of the barracks floors, but almost every work task we were given.

We got used to the pressure of the routine. And, we accepted it as we began to realize that the DI was taking guys from every type of background -- upbringing, beliefs and attitudes -- and converting them from a random collection of individuals into the beginnings of a team whose members would not abandon each other in the heat of battle.

And just so we didn't think we were learning everything quickly and easily, the DI's would bring us down to earth by pointing out our stupid mistakes. Their name for those of us who displayed learning disabilities for Marine tactics was "S__t Bird." Everyone was christened with this nickname sometime during the course of boot camp – whenever they earned it, which was usually often.

To remove a little of the frustration brought on by all the hard work, we would have boxing matches – using gloves. We would be paired off, and the match would only last until someone went down. This wasn't by knockout. We'd box on the beach, and the footing in the soft sand wasn't good. In one match, I drew my right hand way back, and as my opponent followed that hand -- I hit him with my left and knocked him off balance. He tripped in the sand and went down. The DI's would keep an eye on us and call a match if it got out of hand – or if we were not trying to make a real effort of it.

They would drill us all over the place – including the beach. There were sand fleas everywhere. One favorite DI act was to have us stand at attention – knowing that the sand fleas would fly into our ears -- buzzing and biting. And the DI would relish our torment and say, "You had your chow this morning, now let them have theirs."

There were a lot of little annoyances like that, but I thought they were funny in a way. And yet, I knew these annoyances were deliberate. Their purpose was to build discipline among us, and to train us to stand and hold fast when commanded to do so.

One of the most difficult exercises in boot camp was the running of the bayonet course on the rifle range. To execute it, you had to run this course in under so many seconds. I had run this course 2 or 3 times before the final attempt. I wasn't sure I was ready.

The day I ran the course for my test, the Captain in charge of the bayonet drill was upset because things were not going well. The course included having to do a parry right and a parry left, and then hit the heads of two dummies in sequence – one with the bayonet and the other with the butt of the rifle. You finished by raising your rifle and pretended to get off two shots. As I stood in line waiting for my turn, I watched how the guys ahead of me ran it – especially their footwork in doing the parries. I had my set all planned out. I knew I was a good runner, and I ran that course as hard as I could.

When I had finished, I heard the captain say, "Get that man's name!" I thought I was in big trouble for something I did or didn't do. Then I heard the Captain say to everyone, "That's the way I want to see you other guys do it!"

After several weeks, our hair had grown out from the near-scalping we got when we first arrived at Parris Island. This time, we got haircuts that were short – but neatly trimmed. The barber was in a bad mood because he was working alone. Another barber was to have been there – but he didn't show up. I knew I was taking a chance, but I told him I could cut hair and offered to help. He looked at me as if he didn't know whether to believe me or not, then he took me up on my offer. He seemed pleased with my work, and I cut his work load considerably. When all the other recruits were done, he cut my hair – and gave me a professional cut. It was a better haircut than any of the other guys got, and they teased me about it. But, the barber gave it to me as a reward – because he felt that I had earned it.

I made Private First Class out of boot camp – one of only 18 out of 72 who did so. I think the good marks I received in the bayonet drill helped me make it. I also believe that the physical training I received in my Junior and Senior High Schools helped to get me in really good shape for the Marines. And, the training skills of Platoon Staff Sgt. Ratliff and Cpl. Certa were another reason I did well.

There was a guy in the daily lineups named Howie Prince. (Not his real name.) He was a short guy – with blond hair. With all his hair cut off, he looked like a chick straight out of the incubator. The resemblance was so obvious that all the guys began to call him Chick. It was an apt nickname – and it stuck. He had an annoying habit of worming into conversations among small groups of close friends. I guess he had a strong desire of wanting to belong to any group that would have him. He was not an easy guy to warm up to. And, he did look real young to us all.

One day, Staff Sgt. Ratliff asked him, "How old are you?" Chick said, "I'm 17." Ratliff said, "You don't look 17." Then Chick said, "My dad died, and my mother signed my enlistment papers." (You could enlist at 17 if one of your parents signed for you.)

But, Chick didn't know that the Marine censors read our mail – coming and going. So, he wrote a letter to this girl he liked -- to tell her that he wanted to take her out on a date when he came home on furlough at the end of boot camp. She wrote to him and said that her mother wouldn't let her date -- because she was only 14. Then he wrote back to tell her that it wasn't a big deal -- because he was only 16.

The censors caught this and confronted him with the lie. By this time we had finished our training. Instead of discharging him, they sent him to a new assignment with a platoon in Hawaii. We didn't hear where he was finally assigned, but it was probably to some lesser support role on a Marine base – probably until he had turned 17.

I came home for my 10 day furlough after boot camp to find that my brother-in-law, Joe Rizzuto, had also enlisted in the Marines. He left for Parris Island during my furlough. My sister Josephine and I saw him off on the train in York. He was another Marine enlistee in the family, and I wished him luck.

When my 10 day furlough was over, I reported to the Marine Corps Air Station at Cherry Point, North Carolina. This base included a staging center for Marines who were being sent to new assignments. There I was selected to go to the Marine Air Squadron Ordnance School in Norman, Oklahoma. I was sure that this was because of my machine shop training in high school. There was always a need for people who had demonstrated the mechanical skills to do ordnance work.

Chapter 4

Marine Aviation Ordnance School – Norman, Oklahoma

At Cherry Point, they put us on a train to Norman. Again, there were no bunks, and we had to sleep on the seats as best we could. It was a three-day trip. The only bright spot on the way happened in what I remember was Mississippi. The train stopped at a station, and these women volunteers had sandwiches and drinks for us. This was just one example of how the folks were really supporting the troops. If I remember correctly, the women had made the sandwiches. It may seem a small thing to some today, but after 2 or 3 days on that train, we really appreciated it.

We started our training with the basic armaments for Marine aircraft -- machine guns, bombs and rockets. We fired the machine guns from pits on the firing range. We had to learn how they worked, and to learn what to do to repair them when they jammed. And they did jam -- because the instructors would rig them to jam. And we had to find the problem wherever it was in the fire, recoil, or reload cycle. Then we had to correct it on the spot with the proper adjustments or replacement parts.

If the problem was a faulty part, we had to make a replacement part using only hand tools that were likely to be available in the field – hacksaws, files, hand drills, and emery cloth. I was asked to make a replacement cam for the automatic reloading mechanism of a machine gun. I used my machine shop background and made a cam, and polished it to a shine with emery cloth. When I showed it to the instructor, he looked at me and said, "Where did you get this?" I simply said, "I made it." I'm still not sure whether he believed me or not. (I have always been grateful to my father for giving me skilled hands.)

We gradually learned the other skills required for working with aircraft armaments at Norman. We worked with obsolete planes and equipment, but the principles were the same. We advanced to working with the bomb fuses and detonators, and learned how they had to be installed and removed. (Very carefully!)

One day an Instructor came into our barracks and said, "We need 50 guys to volunteer to be aircraft gunners." I volunteered – because being a gunner was something I really wanted to do. But, they gave us a month of mess duty instead. When the month was up, the instructor came into the barracks again – and asked for 50 more volunteers to be aircraft gunners. Having been burned the first time, I did not volunteer. Naturally, they gave the gunner job to the new guys.

One day, Bud Swartz (not his real name) suggested we learn how to box. I agreed – and we put on the gloves. Well, he began to beat on me with a flurry of punches that told me that he already knew how to box. It turned out that I was being pummeled by a guy from New York who had trained as a professional boxer! He said he was taking it easy on me. I called the match. I wanted to learn to box – not keep him in shape for his fellow boxers back in New York.

We would sometimes go into Oklahoma City on the bus for liberty. It was about 18 miles from Norman. One time, five of us sat on the wide, bench-type rear seat at the back of the bus. About 3 or 4 seats forward of us sat a colored woman. In the bus there was a sign that read, "All colored to the back of the bus." We saw the sign, but we were a gang of Marine buddies who were going on the town. We had attitude -- and we were not going to move in response to the bus driver's request to obey the sign. The colored woman broke into a big smile, and the bus driver kept looking back at us. We told the driver that we weren't moving. We figured that he wasn't going to stand up to 5 Marines. For whatever reason, he let us be. The colored woman kept smiling, and she was on top of the world. This was the way it was in 1944 – even with the war.

Norman was actually a Navy base. We'd sometimes march on the grounds, and sailors would hang out of the windows of their barracks and call us names. And, our DI – a guy named Gorski -- would halt us in front of their barracks and say, "Go get 'em." We would run towards the barracks, and then they'd run from the windows toward the doors. But, our DI would always call us back before there was a brawl.

There was a bar in Oklahoma City named "Daisy Mae's". Daisy Mae was the long-suffering girl friend of the newspaper comic strip hero, "Li'l Abner". The waitresses were all dressed like Daisy Mae – in short black skirts and blouses with large red polka dots. Both were tattered at the edges in the style of the hillbilly women of the comic strip village of "Dogpatch".

But I never went into Daisy Mae's. It had swinging doors. And those doors were constantly flying open – and there would be a Sailor and a Marine coming out fighting. That was sort of funny to see, but I didn't go in there because these were just sort of traditional scuffles between Sailors and Marines – sort of a sibling rivalry.

I was saving my fight for combat zones – and those wonderful guys who gave us Pearl Harbor.

Chapter 5

Marine Aviation Squadrons VMTB 143 and 232 -- Santa Barbara, California

The course at Norman was only the first step in learning Marine aircraft ordnance. When it was over, they sent us to a Marine base in San Diego to be assigned to the next level of Marine Air Ordnance instruction. Again, we had a long and tiring rail trip from Norman to San Diego – passing through Texas, New Mexico, Arizona, Nevada and California.

At San Diego, I was assigned to Squadron VMTB – 143, which was located in nearby Santa Barbara. (V stands for fixed wing aircraft, MTB stands for Marine Torpedo Bomber, and 143 is the squadron number.)

We learned to arm the Grumman "Avenger" torpedo bomber. Affectionately known as the "Turkey", it was a large, single engine plane that could carry either torpedoes or various types of bombs or depth charges – even jelly gas (napalm) canisters. It carried a crew of 3: the pilot, a rear-facing ball-turret gunner, and a bottom tail gunner/radio operator. It could fly from land bases and carrier decks. It could attack enemy ships with torpedoes from 50 feet above sea level or dive bomb ships or land targets from altitude. It could strafe and bomb enemy airstrips with fragmentation bombs. It could provide close tactical support of Marine and Army ground forces with various size bombs, rockets, and machine gun fire. It could also deliver ammunition, grenades, food, medical supplies and water to front-line troops by dropping parachute packs.

It was the heaviest single-engine plane of World War II. We were going to learn how to service its guns and bomb loads at the Marine Aviation base at Santa Barbara. I would gain a great deal of respect for this rugged, versatile, do-everything aircraft in the months to come.

At this time, my brother-in-law, Joe Rizzuto, was at Camp Pendleton learning to be a parachute rigger. My sister Josephine was staying at the Rosicrucian Lodge in Oceanside – close to Camp Pendleton. Shortly after I arrived at the San Diego facility, I hitchhiked to Oceanside to see my sister. I stayed there overnight – in a $2 room. I hitchhiked back to the base in San Diego the next day. They had roll call in the morning, but I had a buddy answer "here" for me. My luck was holding: They marked me present.

I was getting a reputation as sort of a lucky adventurer. There was a self-proclaimed tough guy from Chicago named Wallace in the group who didn't like me. One day, he told the guys that he was going to wrestle me and take me down. Well, he tried – but he couldn't. Afterwards, he held a grudge against me because I had embarrassed him in front of his buddies. I thought we were just going to have a friendly competition – but he took it far too personally. He never got over it.

I met a guy named Bob Messmer in VTMB – 143, and we became good buddies. We used to go into Santa Barbara and Goleta together to sightsee. At this time, there was a popular song titled, "Drinking Rum and Coca Cola." So, we decided to try this exotic "Cuban" drink. We went into a liquor store in Santa Barbara and bought a bottle of rum. It was illegal to take liquor onto the base. So, I stuck the bottle into my pants and hooked the neck under my belt. I couldn't walk naturally and had to limp. When we walked into the base the guards looked at me with a little bit of curiosity. I guess they thought I was hurt from a fight or a fall, but they didn't bother checking me out. Once safely in our tent, we secured the bottle. There were Coke machines on the base, and we all got Cokes and satisfied our desire to know how rum and Coca Cola tasted. It was good – and we all sang the song to celebrate our luck at not having been discovered.

This adventure was a high-risk violation of base rules. But, I wasn't caught, and I don't know why. And yet, I was always doing crazy things like this. I guess I had this spirit of adventure that just made me curious and willing to take chances to learn more about the world.

There was a side effect to this curiosity. Strangely, my buddies respected me for it. They seemed to think I had a knack for adventure – with the luck of not getting caught. But the really dangerous tests were still to come -- on an island in the northwestern Pacific.

We worked hard at learning how to service the machine guns, rig the various types of bombs in the bomb bay – and set the corresponding fuses and detonators. We were ready to move on to our first field assignment.

One day, they split the group into two parts. Messmer and Renda were on opposite sides of the alphabetical dividing line. Bob remained with Squadron

143, and was assigned to serve on the Escort Carrier "Gilbert Islands".
I was assigned to land-based Squadron 232, the "Red Devil" Squadron. Talk about long shots, this was the same squadron that my York neighbor Tony Ragusa was in! He inspired me to join the Marines – and here I end up in the same squadron. What are the odds?

And, just to keep the coincidence rolling, I ran into Tony a few days after I went to the San Diego base for our next assignment. I was there with Squadron 232 -- waiting to be shipped overseas. On my way to the mess hall, I saw Tony coming out. We stopped and talked – two boyhood friends from Cherry Alley. He was on his way to a new assignment at a Marine Air base in the Mojave Desert. I told him I had my high school yearbook with me, and he asked to borrow it overnight. He returned it the next morning.

(I wanted it back before we shipped out. It would be my "memories of home" guide while I was overseas. I carried it for my entire tour of duty – through the heat and the humidity of the Pacific Theater.)

Chapter 6

Across the Wide Pacific

After a week of waiting at San Diego, we received the news that we were to go to our next assignment. It had to be somewhere in the Pacific Theater: That's where the Marine Avengers were flying. A couple of days later they handed out "next of kin" cards – to get names and current home addresses of our parents or our closest relatives. Bud Swartz, the guy who had surprised me with his boxing skills at Norman, came up to me and asked what these cards were for. He seemed surprised when I told him, and he began to tear up as he turned and walked away. I was curious as to why he was acting this way. We all knew we were to be sent overseas when our training was done.

When they gave us the orders to go overseas, they gave us liberty for the night before shipping out. This was an old tradition. Well, 5 of my buddies elected to go to Tijuana for sex. This was also an old tradition. While they were being served by the shady ladies of Tijuana, one of them changed his mind. I don't know if it was the squalor of the place or what. The girl told him she couldn't give back his money, but she told him to at least give her a kiss – and that would satisfy house rules. He managed to keep this misadventure to himself on the trip back to San Diego.

A few days later we were at the docks in San Diego waiting to ship out. There was a long ramp leading up to the troopship. We walked up the ramp – which was wide enough so that we could walk with our seabags and rifles without bumping into each other. I had seen ship departures in the movies, and they were fun events. People on the dock were waving to their departing friends and relatives standing at the ship's rail – and they were waving back. There were shouted goodbyes, smiles, confetti and balloons. That was the movie version.

Our departure was nothing like that. The people gathered at the dock were quiet, and there were no smiles. A troopship is not a luxury liner full of beautiful people bound for a European vacation. The people on this San Diego dock were saying goodbye to sons, brothers, husbands, and fathers that they might never see again. (Some may have seen the recent grim newsreels of the many dead Marines washing back and forth in the surf at Tarawa.)

For some unknown reason, Bud Swartz did not board the Sea Ray with us. Whether he got an emergency leave to visit a dying parent – or just went AWOL – we didn't know.

Our ship was the Sea Ray, an attack transport that could carry about 1,700 troops with their equipment. She was about 450 feet long and could make 18 knots. There were 25 Higgins landing craft nested and stacked on deck.

Our first meal onboard the Sea Ray was hash and bread – and the bread had weevils in it. For the first couple of days you picked the weevils out. They were baked into the bread – so some digging was necessary. Then, the traditional taunt arose from some veteran at the table: "What's the matter: Don't you like meat with your bread?" So, you closed your eyes and you ate. You've got to be a tough Marine – you can't be seen picking out anything as harmless as weevils.

After a few days at sea, the secret of the lone abstainer of the Tijuana 5 got out somehow -- and the other 4 guys ridiculed him without mercy. But, he who laughs last, laughs loudest. The 4 who had taken full advantage of the $2 entry fee began to have difficulty urinating. The recently–introduced drug Penicillin came to the rescue. The infected 4 were given a shot a day for 5 days. The ridicule died away, and the 4 added Tijuana to their list of lessons learned.

As we were passing Hawaii, a Japanese submarine was sighted, and it began to trail us. The Sea Ray was a new troopship and could go 18-20 knots. At that time, the fastest subs could only go about 15 knots on the surface – and they were much slower when submerged.

Because of the Japanese sub threat, we had to go below decks every night and sleep in watertight compartments. These compartments would be sealed by closing the doors and hatches. It felt like there was no air circulating in these compartments. The idea was, that if the ship were torpedoed, only the torpedoed compartments would flood -- but the ship wouldn't sink. The sealed compartments would keep the ship afloat. But, if you were in a breached compartment, you were in fact entombed – and in danger of being drowned. I remember that it got so hot in those compartments that we all had to sleep in the nude. After 3 days, we outran the sub – and they let us go back to normal sleeping arrangements.

We steamed south and crossed the equator. Those of us that who were crossing the equator for the first time were called "Pollywogs". And we had to be initiated by those on board who had crossed before. They had a guy dressed as King

Neptune who sat in a chair and presided over the initiation ceremony. They rounded us up, and because there were no women on board, we had to strip off all our clothes. Then they either cut off all our hair, or cut a strip or patch in the middle. They covered us with battleship gray paint, and paddled our behinds. At the end of this entertainment, they turned the fire hoses on us. These were high pressure hoses -- and the streams were knocking us down. We turned away from the hoses to protect our eyes – and other vulnerable parts.

Aside from the whacking we took from the high-pressure hoses, we received what can best be described as an extreme enema. As soon as the water was directed away from us, we raced to the head to relieve ourselves. Men fought to get to the commodes. It was an ugly scene and one I never want to repeat.

There were some guys who tried to hide in the hold of the ship to avoid all this fun, but the crossing vets went down and got the dodgers. The vets then worked them over pretty good.

Many of the guys would pass the time on the Sea Ray by playing cards – mostly blackjack. I never learned to play cards, so I passed my time standing at the bow of the ship watching the flying fish. They would leap out of the water and sail through the air ahead of the ship on their long pectoral fins. It amazed me that they could stay airborne for as long as they did. And, there were so many of them. I would watch them for hours.

We had to take salt water showers on board the Sea Ray. They gave us salt water soap, but you felt sticky when you were done – like you hadn't had a shower at all. So, we'd borrow another guy's helmet, and fill it and our helmet with fresh water at the drinking fountain. With one helmet of water we'd soap up – and with the other we'd rinse off. After a while the Sea Ray's crew got wise and told us that was against regulations. They were running out of fresh water from the storage tanks, and they had to produce drinking water from seawater with the onboard desalination plant.

There were ropes that hung down from the deck of the ship to the water line. If the order to abandon ship was given, we were to climb down these ropes. When our white clothes needed washing, we would tie them to the bottom ends of these ropes and drop them into the ocean. We'd let them drag in the seawater for about 15 minutes. When we pulled them out, they were washed clean and bleached white from the salt water. We'd set them out to dry, and they were soon ready to wear again.

We continued to steam south and west for about 3 weeks and docked at Guadalcanal in the Solomon Islands. The fierce battle for Guadalcanal in 1942 – where the Japanese were halted and turned back from their invasion of the Solomons – had been over more than a year. But the beaches still showed the broken palm trees, bomb craters, smashed equipment and other debris from the intensity of this key battle. I had some colored pencils and the Red Cross stationery with me, and I stood at the rail of the Sea Ray and made a sketch of the beach. Tony Ragusa had fought on Guadalcanal at Henderson Field. He was an airplane mechanic for VMSB – 232, sleeping under his plane at night to protect it from the Japanese infiltrators who would sneak in and try to blow up our planes.

The Sea Ray was anchored at Guadalcanal for 3 days. It was hot, and I wanted to go swimming. The Naval officers would not let their sailors go swimming. They said there was a danger because there were sharks and barracuda in the water. They said the barracuda could take a bite out of you as they swam by. But the Marine officers said it was OK if we wanted to swim. So, my buddy Donald Neild and I dove in. As we were swimming, the tide began to pull us away from the ship! We were in good shape, but we really had to swim hard to get back.

The next day, I was standing at the rail looking into the water. Suddenly, I saw a 12 foot-long shark laying alongside the ship. That put an end to my swimming at Guadalcanal. I didn't go in even from the shore. I heard that sharks would come after you in the surf as well as offshore. The Naval officers knew what they were talking about when they wouldn't let their guys go in.

Following the shark sighting, some sailors told us the lore of porpoises. You felt pretty good when you saw porpoises. They said that they would butt the sharks to death. And, they seemed to like humans. We heard that if they would find men in the sea they would push them to the shore. I don't know whether or not that's true, but they would swim alongside our ship for hours. It almost seemed like they knew we were friendly to them.

Not long after the shark sighting, I was standing at the rail alongside a short, blond-haired guy who was an aircraft mechanic with the Squadron. I didn't know his name because we usually stuck with our own group. I knew he was one of the more active gamblers.

He had 20 silver dollars, and he was dropping them into the water one at a time. The water was so clear that you could watch his silver dollars flip and swoop as they tumbled toward the bottom. I asked him what he was doing. He said, "I ain't going to carry those things with me, they're too darn heavy." You ran into some crazy guys in the service. During the depression, those 20 silver dollars would have been a fortune to me.

Then we left Guadalcanal and steamed across the channel to Tulagi – a smaller island that had once been the capitol of the Solomon Islands. We then headed east to the New Hebrides Islands. It had taken 18 days to reach this point from San Diego – including the 3 or 4 day stop at Guadalcanal.

Chapter 7

The New Hebrides

Espiritu Santo was one of the main islands in the New Hebrides group. The beach was like a travel poster for a tropical paradise. In fact, it is the locale of James Michener's book, "Tales of the South Pacific" -- better known from the stage and film musical versions, "South Pacific." As we docked there, the water was so clear we could see all these black and white striped fish swimming around the ship.

"Santo" had been a frontline Navy base during the fierce battles for the Solomon Islands in 1942. It was from Santo that Major Greg "Pappy" Boyington led his Black Sheep squadron of Marine Corsair fighter planes against the Japanese. His attacks included raids against their main South Pacific fortress at Rabaul on the island of New Britain.

As the war progressed and the Japanese were driven back from Guadalcanal, Santo became a rear guard base. It had a harbor and an airstrip, and it was now used as a supply base. Marine units that had served their time in the Pacific Theater were assigned there for recovery from battle before being given either a new assignment or rotation back to the States.

Likewise, Marines entering the Pacific Theater were assigned there to relieve their predecessor squadrons – and to become acclimated to the Pacific Theater environment. As one of these handoffs, we were sent there to relieve the current VMTB – 232 Squadron. They had just completed their tour of duty in the Solomon Islands and were awaiting return to the States for regrouping and retraining.

And were they happy to see us! They hugged us -- we were their ticket home! They were tanned, rugged and ragged. What was left of their uniforms was bleached from the sun, and their trouser legs had frayed and been cut short. The heat, torrential rains, and seaside humidity of the islands in the south Pacific are hard on men, clothing, and equipment. (These "features" of the islands are not included on the travel posters.)

One of the vets asked if there was anyone in the replacement group that did art work. One of our guys – remembering the sketch I had made of the beach at Guadalcanal -- said, "Yeah, Frank does." So, this homeward-bound vet gave me all his drawing pencils and paper.

The 232 vets took us back to an area of coconut groves where the tents were. Together with the beach, the coconut groves did make "Santo" look like a typical south-seas tropical isle. We began to settle in. Towards evening, these huge bats – they looked to be the size of eagles – began swooping down on us from the trees. Some of our new arrivals began shooting at these giant bats.

The 232 vets quickly said, "Don't shoot them! They eat the bugs. Just let them go. They won't bother you." Well, they had been living on Santo and knew the territory – so we quit shooting. I came to find out that these were fruit bats of the south western Pacific area. And, yes, they really had wingspans of 5 to 6 feet! Some people called them flying foxes because of their long muzzles and pointed ears.

(Saying that these bats were the size of eagles is not an exaggeration. The next time you watch the movie, "The Bridge on the River Kwai" [Best Picture, 1957], look for the scene where thousands of these bats are flushed out of the treetops by the gunfire between the British and Japanese patrols. Their huge swarms are truly amazing!)

The next delightful local animals we met were the coconut crabs. They were jet black – and could crack coconut shells with their powerful claws. (Some people said the coconut had to be cracked from the impact of having fallen from the tree, but we believed they could crack it whole.) The 232 vets told us to watch where we put our feet when we rolled out of our beds in the morning. These crabs could take off toes in an instant.

And, I can't forget the blowflies. They were the size of stateside horseflies – but they bit harder. I don't know why they called them blowflies, you couldn't blow them off. They would get on you and keep biting. You had to brush them off with your hands.

We slept on cots covered with netting to keep the mosquitoes from biting us. Malaria was a problem everywhere in the South Pacific. And, the rats would run along the netting from one cot to the next. We tried to sleep in the middle of the cot – to keep from getting bitten.

We were given some group instructions in a plywood "PB" hut regarding what we had to do -- and what we didn't have to do – to provide ordnance services to our planes. One day while we were in this hut, we heard a low rumble -- followed by continuous "bang, bang, bang" noises. We thought the Japanese were attacking us. We ran out of the hut – and had trouble keeping our balance because the ground was moving. An earthquake was shaking the island, and the coconuts were falling from the trees and raining down on the ground and on the hut. It was a natural barrage of coconuts. One guy got hit on the head – and it broke his neck and killed him. The rest of us made it back into the hut without being hit. But it was an introduction to the way nature can behave in the island paradises of the Pacific Theater.

On the island were two types of native peoples. The Polynesians were tan and lived close by the sea. We didn't see much of them once we were away from the beach and into the coconut groves.

We were surprised one day in the groves when a tribe of aborigines appeared out of the jungle at our tents. They were small – none taller than 5 feet, and they were the blackest people I had ever seen. They had hair like native Africans, and they had small white bones through their noses. They must have ended up in the New Hebrides after some long-ago migration from Africa.

After our initial surprise at their arrival, they made us understand that they wanted to trade the bananas they had brought for the empty 5 gallon coffee cans we usually discarded. We guessed that they used them to catch and carry rainwater. So, we made the trade – and they disappeared into the jungle. We wouldn't see them again for days – until they wanted more cans. Then they'd return to carry on the trading. We really enjoyed the bananas – and they were good neighbors.

There was a dormant volcano on Santo. The crater cone was filled with crystal-clear water. You could look down into the water and see the lava formations at the bottom. We hung ropes from the surrounding treetops, and we would swing out on them and dive into the pool. We didn't have bathing trunks. But, this was a tropical paradise – and it was just plain kid fun for us all.

I liked to swim under water, and I tried to find the bottom of that pool. I'd go down and down until it felt like my ears were about to burst – and I had to come up. I never did find out how deep the water was.

Our behavior at the volcanic pool fascinated the aborigines. They had a high rope bridge strung across the middle of the pool. When we were there, they would line up on this rope bridge to watch these crazy, naked Marines do their swing-and-dive games. Perhaps they thought we would awaken the volcano god, and they didn't want to miss the show when he steamed us alive as punishment for disturbing his sleep.

We didn't get much food on Santo. We were fed twice a day, and most of the time it was hash. Then, the cooks got some shredded lamb tongues from New Zealand. And, they weren't bad. There was one problem. We had a couple of farm boys in the squadron who were familiar with sheep. They decided to have some fun with us city boys. They'd talk among themselves, but loud enough so that we could hear, and they said that they remembered those slimy tongues back on the farm .This caused one of the guys to throw up in his tray. He then walked away – muttering a few choice words about how they had ruined his meal.

But, there is always some comic relief to events – even to stories of bad food. One of our guys, Ottis C. Jones, was at the latrine -- when 2 wild pigs wandered out of the jungle. He killed them both with one shot. The guys dug a pit and Elmer Favinger barbequed them. So, for about 3 days, we had tasty pork meals. They were a welcome relief from the usual hash and K rations.

As part of the training on Santo, they put me on guard duty one night. You had to stay with a plane and learn the feel – the sights and sounds -- of a tropical night in the Pacific. There were no Japanese on Santo, but there would be on the islands we would eventually invade. We were told the Japanese were adept at infiltrating Marine camps at night – especially to kill pilots and blow up airplanes. Tony Ragusa had to sleep at his plane on Guadalcanal to guard it, and we knew it was necessary that we be prepared to do the same.

One day soon after we arrived, they brought a young Marine to me and said he was assigned to be my "assistant." I had not asked for an assistant, and none of the other ordnance guys had one. This guy did not have ordnance training. He was classified as "General Duty" -- which meant he had no training in any special type of work.

I wondered what this association was going to be like. Was this guy a problem that nobody wanted? To add to the puzzle, he was what was then known as an "Indian boy". Did they pass him along because the guys in his outfit didn't want him? Was he a goof off or a screw-up? Or, was it just because he was an Indian? (In the future, he would be known as a Native American. But, as with the woman on the bus in Oklahoma City, this was 1944.)

His name was Willis Knight, and I cautiously began to teach him about the machine guns, bombs and fuses. I was amazed at how quickly he learned everything. I taught him all about the machine guns: how to take them apart, how to adjust the spacer to set the bolt, how it would slide forward, how it would fire, how the shock of the recoil would throw it back, and how it would pick up the next round and bring it forward to repeat the cycle until you released the trigger.

In the bomb bay, there were 10 shackles that held the bombs. You could install a 2,000 pound torpedo, or 10 – 100 pound bombs, or 6 – 260 pound bombs, or

4 – 500 pound bombs, or a 1,000 or 2,000 pound bomb. You could also install a canister that held 1,000 pounds of napalm -- jellied gasoline. He learned how to install 6 depth charges for anti-submarine missions. And, he learned how to rig the parachute packs that contained food and water, small arms ammo, grenades and medical supplies that would be dropped to frontline Marine infantry units. Knowing how to rig some of these loads was almost an art form, but he got it right away.

I also taught him how to fuse the bombs. He had a knack for the work and became an excellent ordnance man. I was relieved -- and so glad to have him. (My luck was still holding.) We became the best of buddies, and he worked with me until the end of the war.

One day, Willis asked me if I would give him a haircut. I said, "Sure, why not?" He said,"Back in Muskogee, they won't cut my hair. They told me my hair is different." So I said, "Well, your hair is no different from other peoples' – except it is coal black. In fact, it is so black there are strands of blue in it." But at that time, many people, including me, didn't know that the ancestors of Native Americans migrated to North America from parts of Siberia – and had many Asian characteristics.

One day a small group of us went on an exploratory patrol into the jungle. We came across some wild horses – probably descended from domesticated horses brought by the French planters. We spooked them and they began to scatter. There was a mare with a foal who stood her ground and began to menace us. In respect for the wild mother protecting her young, we backed off. But the jungle was so thick we could barely get through the trees. It wasn't long until we were lost. After several hours of wandering, Sergeant Tabaka asked if anyone could figure out how we could get back to where we came in.

I said I thought I could – because I remembered that the sun was in front of us when we entered the jungle. By then the sun was starting to set behind us, so I said we should go towards where the sun had come from. We tried it, and we got back to right where we came in. Once again, my luck was with me.

There was an old fire truck near our camp left over from the French colonial administration days. It was rusted out, and the sides were only spot-welded to the frame. Some evenings they would show a movie in another area of the island. We'd jump onto this fire truck and ride to where the movie was set up. The ride had some thrills. The spot-welded sides would swing out when we went around curves. I remember hanging on -- and you could feel the sides moving in and out. We hoped that the sides wouldn't tear off as we sped through the curves in the coconut grove roads.

We'd arrive at the "theater" – a screen and some sort of platform. As primitive as it was, we looked forward to these movie nights. It gave us some entertainment -- and a Hollywood-type glimpse of home. They used the platform for church services on Sunday.

We had been on Santo for about a month, and we were getting accustomed to the climate and to each other. It was time to go north to take over the ordnance duties of the VMTB -232 Squadron in a combat zone.

Chapter 8

The Big Lagoon

At Santo we boarded the troopship Cape Cleare to begin the second leg of our Pacific voyage. Our destination was the large atoll of Ulithi in the western Caroline Islands. Its main feature was the immense lagoon inside the atoll ring. The Japanese had been using it for several years to assemble fleets to support their conquest of the Philippines, Southeast Asia, and the South Pacific. Now it was our turn to capture this prize lagoon and use it to assemble our fleets and take the war to several key Japanese islands in the western Pacific -- and to the Japanese mainland. We were finally going in harm's way.

The Cape Cleare was actually built for, and crewed by, the Merchant Marine Service. The decks were not as orderly as on the Sea Ray, and her crewmen were not dressed as neatly as the Navy crewmen. These Merchant Mariners did wear uniform tops, but their pants were blue jeans.

I especially remember one crewman. He was tall and had long, black curly hair. He had one blue eye and one brown eye – and wore an earring. He was part of the crew that manned the 5 inch gun on the fantail during defensive drill. He looked like a pirate. But, appearances aside, he and all the other crewmen really knew their stuff.

Later I would learn that the Merchant Marine suffered the highest casualty rate of all of the services that fought in World War II. They crewed the ships that carried the supplies of war, and these cargo ships were targeted by enemy ships, planes and submarines in every theater. They didn't get many headlines, but I hope they got the gratitude and respect they deserved.

The Cape Cleare partly retraced our Sea Ray route -- sailing west past the New Hebrides and the Solomon islands. After passing Bougainville and Emirau, she turned north toward Peleliu – then east toward Ulithi. This route was relatively safe from Japanese attackers. The voyage took about 30 days.

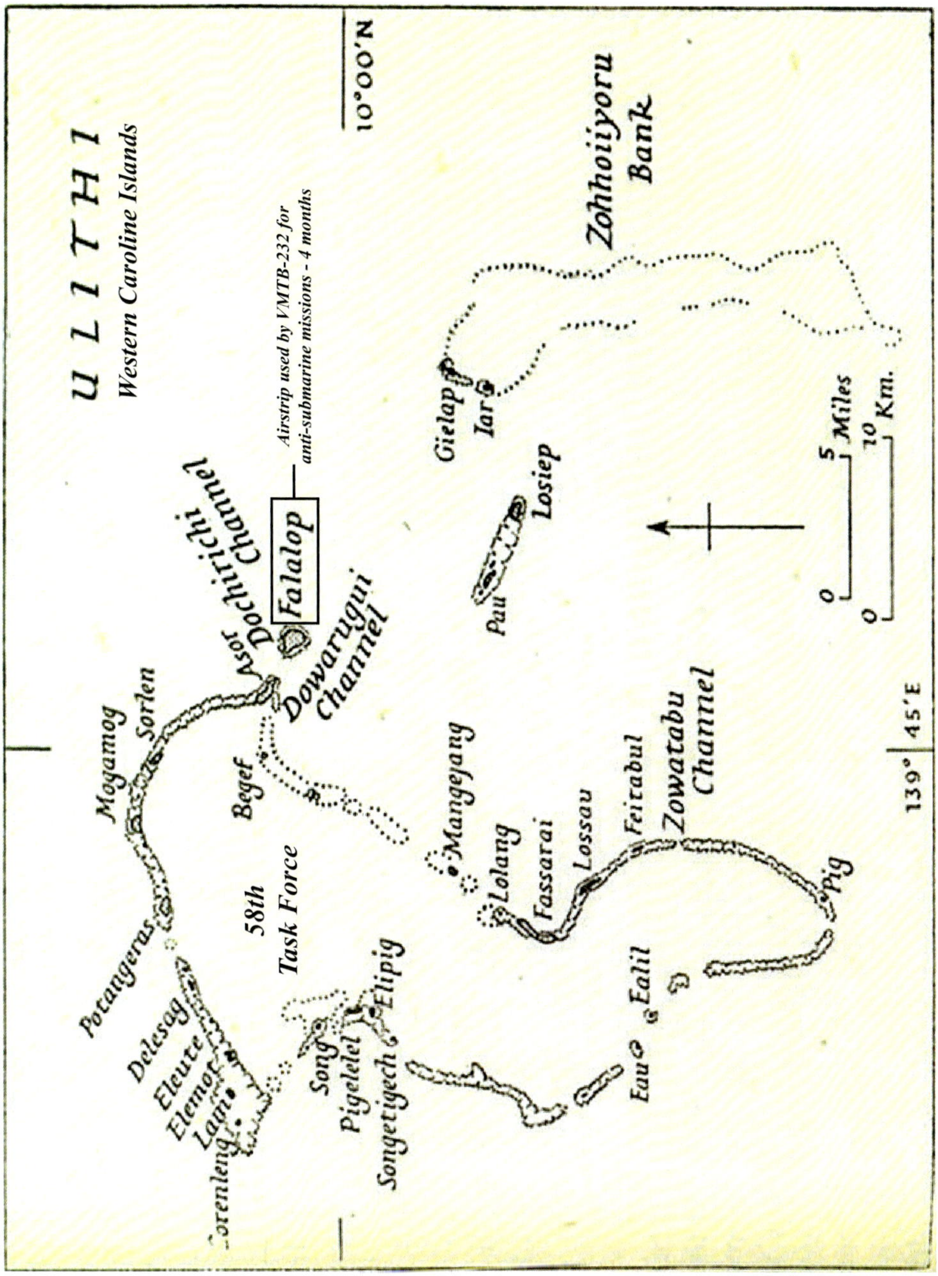
ULITHI
Western Caroline Islands
Airstrip used by VMTB-232 for anti-submarine missions - 4 months
Falalop
Dochirichi Channel
Asor
Dowarugui Channel
Sorlen
Mogamog
Potangeras
Delesag
Eleute
Elemoi
Lam
Sorenleng
58th Task Force
Begef
Song
Pigelelel
Songetigech
Elipig
Mangejang
Lolang
Fassarai
Lossau
Feitabul
Zowatabu Channel
Pig
Ealil
Eau
Pau
Losiep
Gielap
Iar
Zohhoiiyoru Bank
0 5 Miles
0 10 Km.
10°00'N
139° 45'E

Before we arrived at Ulithi, the Navy had shelled the larger islands to prepare them for the Marine invasion forces. But, the Japanese had gone before the Navy got there. They had apparently withdrawn their forces to Yap -- an island fortress with several airfields only 100 miles from Ulithi. The Japanese probably thought that they could attack Ulithi at any time from their well-defended airbases on Yap.

The naval bombardment of the islands of Ulithi had knocked down a lot of coconut trees, and – unfortunately -- resulted in a few civilian casualties. One of those killed was the chief's daughter. The chief was naturally saddened by his loss. To relieve his grief, they gave him his first-ever airplane ride -- and showed him his kingdom from the air.

Ulithi is the largest atoll in the Caroline Islands – and features one of the largest deep harbor lagoons in the world. It has 4 small islands and 40 islets in the coral ring. It looks like a necklace that is 20 miles long and 10 - 15 miles wide

The largest of the 4 islands is Falalop. It is the pendant of the necklace – and sits near the northeast corner of the atoll. It is only one-half square mile in area, but it is large enough for an airstrip – and the Japanese had constructed one. The Naval Construction Battalion (N.C.B., or SeaBees) set to extending it so that it reached across the island – beach-to-beach. It was to be the home of Squadron VMTB – 232 for 4 months.

The big attraction of Ulithi for the Navy was the lagoon. It had an anchorage with an average depth from 80 to 100 feet – and it could hold at least 700 ships! It was an ideal place for the Navy to anchor, refuel, and otherwise prepare the largest invasion fleet ever to be assembled.

We didn't know it at the time, but Ulithi was a secret base. During our occupation, the SeaBees and other construction services built piers, ship repair facilities, and materials resupply facilities that could serve the entire Pacific fleet. They even towed a dry-dock to Ulithi from the states that was large enough to lift dry a 45,000 ton battleship. Six thousand welders, ship fitters, carpenters and electricians arrived to build and maintain this vast sea base. It was strategically removed from Pearl Harbor, San Diego and the other shipyards on the west coast of the U.S. It would not be long before the wisdom of this strategy would pay off.

Ulithi is only about 9 degrees of latitude north of the equator. The native women of Ulithi dressed for the year-around 120 degree-plus heat. They wore skirts that they made from palm fronds or awning material, and they were topless. To prevent the possibility of any more civilian casualties, they moved the native population to other islands south and east of the atoll.

(That was the official reason: We all guessed that the brass thought that the presence of all those topless women would distract the men.)

What was left of the native population to entertain us were the large native lizards. They were about 4 feet long with a long, skinny tail. They were harmless to humans. The guys would lift them up and pose for photos. When the photo shoot was over, the lizards would climb up a coconut palm. The only harm they'd cause us was when the very young ones would fall out of a tree and land on your back. You got a prickling sensation when they held on to you with their claws before they would drop to the ground.

The native houses on Falalop were built on stilts made from coconut tree trunks. The stilts were probably to protect the houses from being swamped during storm surges. I guess that a people who could migrate a thousand miles or more over open water in an outrigger canoe could also learn how to build dwellings that could survive the tropical storms that periodically hit the islands.

Not long after we landed on Falalop, Staff Sgt. George Hoover said he had forgotten something on the Cape Cleare. He asked me if I would go along with him to pick it up. I was always game for an outing, so I said that I would go. We hitched a ride on a Navy inter-isle commuter boat to get to the ship.

Sgt. Hoover retrieved his bundle, but when the guy with the boat came to get us, he said he couldn't make the return run to Falalop anymore that day. He had to drop us off at a different island, and he said the mail boat would come by in the morning to pick us up and take us back.

So, he dropped us off at this other island in the Ulithi atoll. There were no US forces there, and it suddenly occurred to us that there might still be some Japanese stragglers hiding in the coconut groves on that island. We didn't know what the night might bring. As a precaution, we slept on the beach -- with our rifles at the ready.

The next morning, a small boat did come by and picked us up. After that adventure, I was more cautious before I would agree to go somewhere strange. Spending the night on that beach with the sand fleas dining on us was enough to cure me. (But, I remained eager to wander when it was my idea – and if I knew in advance where the enemy might be.)

We set up our ordnance operations at the enlarged airstrip on Falalop, and our Avengers began to fly missions. Their primary missions were anti-sub patrol – to find and sink Japanese submarines that were trying to infiltrate the lagoon to threaten the ever-growing number of ships of Task Force 58.

For these anti-sub missions we would load the bomb bay with 6 depth charges –

set to explode at different depths. During these missions, the pilots and gunners of 232 would also be on the lookout for any suspicious ships and small boats. I remember one comic thing about loading depth charges in our Avengers. They were about the shape of oil drums – but of a smaller size. That provided lots of area on which the guys painted "personal" messages to Japanese War Minister Tojo -- and to other Japanese military leaders known to us from Japanese radio broadcasts. The lingo the guys used in these painted messages was the worst of Marine speak, but it allowed the guys to vent against the situation the Japanese had put us in. It was a morale booster, obscenities forgiven.

During one of these bomb bay loadings, one of the guys turned to me and said, "Hey, isn't this where you're from?" I looked, and he was pointing to the hoists that we used to lift the depth charges into the bomb bay. On them it said that they were made in the Naval Ordnance Plant in York, PA. It made me feel good to see that some equipment we were using was made in my home town.

Fortunately, the water was so clear that subs were easily seen from the air. One day, our Avenger crews spotted 2 midget subs trying to enter the lagoon. They sunk one, and radioed the location of the other to the Navy. Before another of our Marine Avengers could get there, the Navy radar crews routed several of their carrier-based Avengers to the second sub – and they sunk it.

Our squadron also flew bombing missions against Yap. The first objective was to bomb the airstrips. The resulting bomb craters would prevent Japanese planes from taking off from Yap to attack our ships and planes at Ulithi – at least until they could fill in the bomb crater. But, the crafty Japanese would fill in the craters with crushed coral – then pour dark oil on top. This made the filled bomb crater look like it hadn't been repaired – both to the naked eye and to the reconnaissance cameras. Like most tricks, this one was eventually discovered. Thereafter, airstrips were bombed whether they seemed cratered or not.

We sometimes armed the Avengers with 1,000 pound napalm canisters for missions to Yap. When they were dropped on the airstrips there, the spreading fireballs from the jellied gasoline would wash over the planes – and damage or destroy many of them.

Unfortunately, 232 lost a pilot on a mission over Yap. We lost another squadron member to a disease that was never identified. The doctor was concerned that it might be some type of plague that would run through the service personnel on Ulithi. This did not happen, and we were spared an epidemic among the highly trained units that were essential to the invasion plans. He was buried on a rise near the end of the airstrip at Falalop – overlooking the Pacific.

The ships of Task Force 58 were beginning to fill the lagoon. They would soon amount to more than 700 ships when the fleet had been completely assembled.

The fleet would include at least 5 fast attack carriers -- and 20 -25 of the smaller escort carriers.

Many Navy fighter squadrons -- and several squadrons of Marine Corsair fighters -- constantly flew protective combat patrols over the lagoon and the nearby areas of the Pacific. They were searching for enemy attack aircraft from Yap or other Japanese bases. Most of these patrol planes were based on the many carriers in the lagoon.

We could see the 5 fast attack carriers and the escort carriers from the beach on Falalop. It was an awesome sight. As time went by, more battleships, cruisers, destroyers, oilers and troop ships continued to enter the lagoon to join Task Force 58.

The shortness of the airstrip on Falalop provided both hazards and entertainment. Many planes would approach to land at too high a speed. If the pilot didn't pull up in time to go around again, he would touch down, overshoot the runway and roll into the Pacific at the far end of the strip. They would have to go out with a mobile crane and lift the plane out of the water -- then bring it back to be checked out.

I remember one 232 pilot, Lt. Brower, started down the runway – but he wasn't taking off. He had forgotten to unfold the wings of his Avenger! He finally realized the problem, turned around and taxied back to try again. When he got back to the starting line, his canopy was open and we could see that his face was beet-red. Everyone was "cheering" him -- and he was really embarrassed.

Movie star Tyrone Power visited Falalop as part of a Marine promotional tour. He piloted a twin engine C–47 transport onto the airstrip. Almost everyone went to see him, but I didn't bother. As far as I was concerned, he was just another Marine doing his job. I had my job to do – and it didn't include gawking at a movie star. He was at Ulithi for only a couple of days – and then he left to continue his tour of the Pacific Theater.

We were on Falalop during Christmas of 1944. President Roosevelt had given a radio chat in which he promised that "all the boys in the services would have a turkey dinner for Christmas." This news was greeted by us with muttered responses of "Yeah, sure." But, when Christmas time came, there were turkeys! I guess the Navy had them, brought them ashore, and were cooking them. Well, we had been on K rations, and the smell from turkeys cooking just drove us nuts.

They had the turkeys stored behind some chicken wire. One guy couldn't stand it. He pulled the chicken wire apart, grabbed a turkey, and ran off with it. Well, they caught him and built a makeshift brig from the same kind of chicken wire and locked him inside.

When the Christmas season began, I noticed that there were some trees on Falalop that looked a little bit like pine trees. I cut one down, got pieces of paper, made paper chains, and hung them on the tree. And everyone in the Squadron was pleased because we had a tree for Christmas. I guess this was just another example of my constant need to be doing some type of art work.

One night around Christmas, I saw the full moon rising out of the Pacific. It was so big, I thought it was going to come down on my head. If you've never seen a full moon rise out of the ocean in the tropics, you can't imagine what it is like.

We used to listen to Tokyo Rose on Falalop. This Japanese-American gal would play American swing music to us. She also had a propaganda pitch designed to demoralize us. She'd say something like, "While you Marines are over here trying to fight a war, your girlfriends and wives back home are running around on you." We listened to and enjoyed the music – which was good. We laughed at the propaganda – which was corny.

I found this little pig that the natives had left behind. I caught him and tried to raise him as a pet. So I put him in the tail gunner's compartment in one of the Avengers. But, he squealed and squealed and wanted out of there. So, I let him go. There were times when you did strange things just to occupy yourself.

We had several USO tours visit us on Falalop. One tour featured a show by Bob Crosby and the 5th Marine Division Band. (Bob's brother, Bing Crosby, was a very popular singer of the day. They still play his recording of "White Christmas" every holiday season.)

We also had a group of Hollywood starlets on a USO tour fly in to entertain the troops. I can't remember if they had a talent show -- or were just there to boost morale by looking pretty. But it ended sadly. Their plane left Falalop – but was never seen again. They must have gone down at sea flying to the next island tour stop – reason unknown.

Our Sgt. Roby found a little sake (rice wine) cask that the Japanese had left behind. He washed it out and put coconut milk inside. He got some sugar from somewhere, put it in the cask, and let it ferment. He got some kind of alcohol from it, and he began to taste the fruit of his labor. It must have been powerful stuff, because he was soon drunk and got a crying jag on. We asked him why he was crying. He would look at us and say, "I don't know why I'm crying, I'm just crying." He didn't share any of this tropical brew with us – which was probably a good thing.

I salvaged a little crate from the things left behind by the Japanese. I put it in our tent and put some of my things on it. The next morning I woke to find myself covered with bedbugs! (They must have missed the last boat to Yap.) Lesson learned: The Japanese had bedbugs. I got rid of the crate and sprayed myself with DDT.

While on Falalop, everyone in our Squadron came down with diarrhea. There was always a 50 foot long line waiting to use the latrine – which we had to dig to deal with the new demand. You no sooner went when you had to get back in line.

There was this little airplane engine mechanic in our group who couldn't wait for his next turn. He fell out of line and began to dig in the sand like a dog would dig – between his legs. Then he squatted down and went in front of everybody. Then he covered it up. Actually, his was the most sanitary way of dealing with the diarrhea.

As a result of this epidemic, they set up some additional outdoor showers. There were sprinkler heads set above a wooden platform with gaps between the boards to allow the water to drain away. We had to shower quickly because we didn't know when we were going to run out of water. It was get wet, soap up, and rinse off.

As to what caused the diarrhea, we felt it had to have been either the food or the water. We got two meals a day, and they weren't really meals. We got something for breakfast, and then about 2 o'clock in the afternoon we got our second meal – and that was it. We didn't have tables to sit at. The meals were served in a big tent, and all around the inside perimeter of the tent was a big board about a foot wide. It served as the food counter, and we stood alongside it to eat our food.

There is no native water on Ulithi, and it didn't rain the 4 months we were there. The water we did have was distilled from sea water, run through rubber hoses, and stored in rubberized Lister bags. It was treated with calcium hypochlorite, and it had both a rubbery and a chemical taste. But, that was the only water there was: We drank it.

Some of our guys went to the weapons tent in an unguarded moment and "requisitioned" several .45 caliber pistols. Fortunately, our officers told us when the weapons guys were going to search our tents for the missing pistols. Being forewarned, our thieves would wrap them and bury them in the sand. The weapons guys would search the tents, but they never found the pistols. I guess that the guys who had taken the .45's eventually took them home in their seabags.

Sgt. Cliff Campbell was a "Plane Captain". His job was to look after the Avengers to see that they were ready for combat. He would check them over to see that nothing was missing or suspicious. And, he would move the Avengers in the absence of the pilots -- if they had to be hidden or to make room for other incoming planes.

One day, he showed me how to move an Avenger. This was a big deal for me. He showed me how to give the engine 2 primes, hit the starter, and run it up to 1,800 rpm for 5 minutes. Then, you had to pull back on the stick just enough to keep the tail wheel from lifting off the ground. (You didn't want to clip the runway with the 13 foot diameter propeller when the tail began to lift.) Then you taxied it wherever you had to go. We didn't fly, but it was a still a thrill for a bomb loader like me to taxi an Avenger – even for only 50 – 100 yards.

If that was my biggest thrill, my smallest was the time a group of us were walking idly through a coconut grove, and a sergeant happened by and saw we were not doing anything at the moment. He did away with our happy mood by telling us to pick up all the coconuts in the grove and put them in a pile.

Soon after we arrived at Ulithi, a dog belonging to Warrant Officer Estes Ratliffe had a litter of 3 "assorted" pups. As soon as they were weaned, Ratliffe gave them up for adoption. I took the rat terrier with an unusual all-black head and a black and white body. My buddies gathered around me and my new dog and asked what I was going to name her.

William Murphy, another member of the squadron, was a tall, good-natured Irishman with a winning smile. He was always talking about his Judy – the girl who was waiting for him back in the states. I thought I'd risk some fun with Murphy, so I said I was going to name the dog Judy – thinking that he would object.

To my surprise, he flashed one of his big smiles, and said he was pleased. My buddies laughed and agreed that Judy would be a good name. This hadn't played out like I thought it would, but changing the name now would create a problem. So, my dog was Judy from then on.

Judy was friendly to all the guys in the squadron. Ulithi was a war zone, and food was scarce. Somehow my buddies and I always managed to find enough scraps to keep Judy well fed.

The next question was how to get Judy to the next base. Unfortunately, dogs belonging to enlisted men were not allowed onboard the troop transport ships. But, Corporal Eli Krueger – a fellow ordnance man in 232 – was to be among those who would remain on Ulithi to service the Avengers until they were moved to the next base.

Eli was a tail gunner and a good friend of mine. He was of German extraction, and he always referred to me as a "spaghetti eater." In the same spirit of fun, I called him a "sauerkraut chugger". He was an avid photographer – and took many photos of 232 guys going about their duties. He also took photos of us in relaxed moments at all our bases. He would mail the film rolls to a photo lab in the States, and they would develop them and send the prints to him at our bases. Eli saw my disappointment at the prospect of losing Judy, and he told me not to worry. He said he would feed and take care of Judy on Ulithi. And, he would bring her to me on an Avenger when they were cleared to fly to the new base. He and Judy would make the trip in one of the Avenger's two gun crew positions.

I was very happy with Krueger's offer. It meant that Judy could continue to be my pet – and a morale booster to the whole squadron at the new base.

After about 4 months on Ulithi, we began to hear rumors that the 232 Squadron was soon to be moved to the next base of operations. Our destination was a secret. Our ground crews were to be transported by troopships. We would land at the new base as soon as an existing airstrip there was secured by the first-ashore invasion force. Our job was to pioneer (prepare) the support facilities at a new airstrip so that it would be ready to service and arm the Avengers when they arrived.

The pilots, gunners and some fraction of the ground crews would remain at Ulithi. They would support the continuing anti-submarine patrols and combat missions to protect the ships in and around the lagoon. They would also continue to support attacks on Yap -- keeping the Japanese busy. The remainder of the ground crews would follow to the new base later on a different troopship – once the new airstrip was operational and we had completed the pioneering of all the supporting services. The pilots and gunners would fly the Avengers to the new airstrip as soon as it was ready. That was the plan.

We all knew that this trip would be different from the previous ones. We would be sailing into a combat zone – and the welcoming committee on the next island would not be friendly Polynesians. The relatively protected life of Ulithi would soon be behind us. The next stop was going to be somewhere close to the Japanese mainland.

The Japanese had learned from their loss of 4 carriers at the battle of Midway that pilot replacement was a process that could take years. They would fight desperately to destroy our pilots and their planes. If they couldn't destroy them in the air, they would try to destroy them on the ground.

Our Ordnance Group – together with the other ground crews – would live only a hundred yards or so from the pilots' tents. That meant that we were close to the planes and pilots, and would be in the airstrip strike zone. We were not going to be frontline infantry troops, but we would get our share of danger from Japanese air attacks – both from aircraft and artillery.

Chapter 9

Sailing into the "Divine Wind"

The lagoon was now filled with the ships of Task Force 58 -- the largest naval task force ever assembled. In addition to the carriers, we could see battleships, cruisers, destroyers, oil tenders, troopships, and landing craft. There were now more than 700 ships gathered, and it was an amazing sight. Task Force 58 was ready to attack the mainland of Japan – and the nearby islands.

At this time, one half of the ground crews of Squadron VMTB – 232 received orders to be ready to leave for a "new" base. Wherever this new base was, it was still in Japanese hands and targeted for invasion. For security reasons, we were not told our destination.

I was in the first echelon of VMTB-232 ground crews to go, and about 250 of us boarded the troopship Freestone. We departed Ulithi in mid-February, 1945. We sailed north in a convoy that followed the spearhead of Task Force 58.

One night, after about two weeks at sea, I heard this "boom, boom" that sounded like naval artillery being fired from battleships and heavy cruisers. We were alongside an island and not far offshore. The Marines must have either landed or were about to land. It was night when we passed by, and we could see a mountain silhouetted by flashes of artillery fire. I asked the guys if anyone knew where we were. One of the sailors in the Freestone crew said the island was Iwo Jima. I thought that was a funny name for an island.

(Later, I came to learn that the island was in fact Iwo Jima. The mountain was Mount Suribachi – the site of the Marine flag-raising made famous by Joe Rosenthal's Pulitzer Prize-winning photograph.)

The next morning, Task Force 58 had continued north on their mission, but the Freestone had turned and sailed southwest. This seemed strange to us: We thought we would continue to go north with the fleet. We guessed there must have been a delay in the invasion plan for our new base -- and that we were being idled in safer waters until the delay was over.

Along the way, we began to see U.S. Navy ships coming from the north. Their masts were blown off, and there was other battle damage visible on the decks, sides and gun turrets. U.S. Navy ships would be providing supporting fire for our ground troops as they were invading islands in the northwest Pacific. We guessed that these damaged ships had been hit by Japanese shore artillery defending their islands under attack. We assumed that our damaged ships were now on their way to the repair shops at Ulithi.

Then we learned that we were approaching Leyte Island in the Philippines. While we were still some distance offshore, 5 Australian military personnel from another ship were transferred to the Freestone. I never learned who or what they were. When we docked at Leyte Island, the Aussies got off the ship. We never saw them again, and we never learned their mission.

We were allowed off the Freestone for 3 days while at Leyte to get our legs back. We wandered around, and exchanged our U.S. dollars for Philippine dollars with local Filipinos. Their money was worthless, but we traded anyway -- just to have souvenirs of our visit there.

Then, we got back on the Freestone and headed for the new base. We were given 2 Atabrine tablets a day to prevent us from getting malaria. These turned our skin and the whites of our eyes yellow. We joked that we hoped that we wouldn't be mistaken for Japs at the new base.

I remember one day during this part of the voyage that the water was the roughest of our entire Pacific experience. I went down to the galley for chow, and when I came back up, I started to walk to my bunk – which was in the bow of the ship and just above the main deck. When I got there, the ship went way down – and then way up again several times. I wasn't seasick often, but this ship motion was really shaking me. The food just shot out of my mouth and onto the deck. I headed for the deck rail – and some guy behind me was yelling at me to "Come back and clean that up!" But, I kept going -- I just had to get to the rail. When I got back, someone had cleaned up after me. (My long-belated thanks to whoever did it.)

Getting enough sleep on the Freestone was a challenge. Our bunks were canvas panels – stretched taut on a tubular metal frame. They were stacked 8 high in the berthing compartments, and climbing into the upper bunks was like a gymnastic exercise. Once you were in your bunk, severe bobbing of the ship would cause the guy in the bunk below to be lifted and banged into the guy in the bunk above. There was a domino effect throughout the stack of bunks.

A steel ship is an oven in the sunbaked tropics – and the onboard steam plant adds to the heat below decks. The ventilation was poor, and, as on the Sea Ray, we all slept in the nude to get some relief.

One way we tried to beat the heat was to nap on deck during the day. The steel decks were too hot, and the best place to nap was on the canvas-covered wooden cargo hatches. We used a triangular buddy system: Three guys would lie down, each with his neck on another guy's ankles for a pillow. I imagined this looked strange from the air, but it worked -- and we got lots of nap time this way.

A crazy event happened on this leg of the voyage. One of the other ordnance guys in 232 – let's call him Rice -- had stolen a pair of large, high-powered binoculars that allowed you to see miles away. We had gone to ordnance school together, and he was an excellent artist.

As we were approaching the target island, he let us look through them. We couldn't see the offshore islands with the naked eye, but they appeared through those binoculars as if by magic.

But, they caught him and put him in the Freestone's brig. It didn't make sense to me why he risked the brig for a key piece of equipment that would be missed almost immediately -- because it would be greatly needed by the Freestone's officers during the approach to the invasion target.

Finally, we arrived offshore at our secret destination. It was the island of Okinawa – about 350 miles south of Japan. It had several airstrips, and we were going to prepare one of them for our Avengers. The Task Force fleet had begun to bombard the island on 24 March – to soften it up before the invasion planned for 01 April.

The plan was that the ground forces would invade the island to capture these several airstrips from the Japanese. Next, the SeaBees would repair the bomb and artillery shell damage that had been inflicted on the airstrips before and during the invasion. According to plan, the Freestone would spend 2 or 3 days holding offshore in the transfer zone while the infantry captured and secured the airstrips. Then, we would be landed to prepare one airstrip to accept our Avengers.

As we approached Okinawa, we had our first look at one kind of defense that was going to be used by the Japanese. We watched as a Japanese plane dove at a ship alongside the Freestone. We thought it was going to drop a bomb on the ship and pull away. Instead, it kept flying and seemed to be deliberately crashed into the side of the ship – killing the pilot.

The resulting explosion blew a hole about 15 by 20 feet in the side of the ship. Luckily, the hole was above the water line. Within 15 minutes, sailors from the ship's repair crews could be seen through the hole, and they began welding steel plates on the side of the ship to close it.

What we had seen was a new and frightening type of warfare. The plane was called a "Kamikaze". It was a suicide attack plane. It was fitted with fixed – not droppable -- explosives, and the pilot stayed at the controls. As his final act, he guided the plane into the target ship.

The Kamikaze plane was a primitive form of a guided missile. The volunteer pilot who flew it knew it would his last mission. The plane had a one-way fuel supply. This was an airborne version of the infamous suicidal "Banzai" charges that Japanese ground forces made earlier in the War.

We hadn't recovered from the shock of this attack when another Kamikaze pilot dove at one of our ships on the other side of the Freestone. But, he overshot it and hit the water. We couldn't tell whether the Navy ack-ack guns had hit the plane and knocked it off course -- or the pilot had misjudged the target.

These two Kamikaze attacks on nearby ships were enough for the Captain of the Freestone. He appeared at the rail of the bridge. I was on deck and heard him yell, "I want these men off this ship!" There was no mistaking the tone of his voice: He meant now – not after the planned 2 or 3 days of holding us in the offshore transfer zone. In addition to the responsibility for his ship and crew, he had the added responsibility for the delivery of the 232 ground crews to the Higgins landing boats. He didn't want us to be caught onboard his ship during another Kamikaze attack. (And, he didn't want the Freestone to be a sitting duck in a holding position in the transfer zone: He had to be free to move offshore so that he could make attack avoidance maneuvers in open water.)

"These men" included us – the first group of ground crews of VMTB – 232. The immediate danger to us was not going to be from the Japanese ground force defenders onshore during the trip aboard our landing craft when we headed for the beach. The Kamikaze pilots of the Japanese Army and Naval Air Forces were not only targeting our carriers and other fighting ships, they were also targeting our troopships!

We ran below decks and got our weapons and other gear – including our 80 pound packs. The crew of the Freestone lowered the Higgins landing boats over the side. We climbed down the cargo nets draped on the sides of the ship and got into the Higgins boats. On the way down, we were careful to not hold onto the horizontal sections of the rope netting – to avoid having someone higher up on the cargo nets from stepping on our hands and skinning our knuckles or breaking our fingers. We also had to time our drop into the Higgins boats so that it was as the top of a wave when we let go. That gave us the least drop distance to the floor of the boat and was easiest on the knees and ankles. We also had to respect the effect of the weight of that 80 pound pack.

As we were scrambling down the nets to enter the Higgins boats, the sailors – in total silence -- stood along the rails of the Freestone to watch us. This reminded me of our departure from San Diego on the Sea Ray. There, the quiet crowd of civilians were watching Marines ship out to the unknown dangers of the Pacific Theater. Here, the sailors who had brought us to invade a Japanese stronghold knew of the high casualty rates suffered by invasion forces during the run to and onto the beach. They were probably wondering how many of us would make it ashore – and what attacks on the Freestone they would undoubtedly face during the battle. The Kamikazes were now every sailor's worst nightmare.

The Higgins boats powered up and ran for the beach – together with a number of Amtracs. (Amphibious tanks). By some miracle, there was almost no fire directed towards us from the shore – just a few mortar shells, and they fell into the water without hitting any boats. As we approached the beach, the Higgins boats slowed. The boat pilots didn't seem to be sure as to how far they could take the boats without hanging them up on the reef. The guys alongside us in an amphibious tank asked us if we wanted a ride. A couple of us said yes, and we swung out of our Higgins boat and onto the Amtrac.

Meanwhile, the Higgins boats continued to approach the beach. They finally slowed and lowered the ramps. The guys onboard surged out, dropped into the water about waist deep, and began to wade in.

But, the amphibious tank driver didn't go in any closer than the Higgins boats. We had to get into the water and wade to shore from waist deep water also. We would have been better off to have stayed with the Higgins boat. (I can't remember if we thanked the Amtrak driver for the ride.)

Sadly, one of our ordnance guys stepped off a Higgins boat and into a hole. As he began to sink, one of his buddies caught hold of his hand. But, with their 80 pound packs and the surf, they couldn't hold on to each other – and he slipped away and was lost.

When we got on the beach, most of our guys holed up in the caves they found there. I found myself alongside a huge shell crater – at least 15 feet deep. Out of curiosity, I crawled into it just to see how deep it really was. Once inside, I thought this wasn't too smart. If a Japanese shell were to fall nearby, it could bury me in beach sand. But, there wasn't any enemy fire coming at us, so I stayed there to wait for orders to advance.

Finally, we were on a Japanese-held island. We were expecting to be in a shooting war – taking fire from small arms, mortars, grenades, artillery shells, and air-dropped bombs. But, there wasn't any incoming enemy fire!

Because of our emergency departure from the Freestone, there were no Marine officers or beach marshals there who were expecting us. As a consequence, we were on our own, and we would have to wait for orders. We expected orders would come when the Infantry beach commanders sorted out the unplanned situation that we found themselves in.

One thing was for certain: We were on Okinawa, and we would have to wait for events to catch up with us.

(Years later, I learned that the name Kamikaze – "Divine Wind" – had originated in the early thirteenth century. On two occasions, Mongols – under Emperor Kublai Khan -- had attempted to invade Japan. Both times, typhoons had destroyed the Mongol fleets just offshore. The Japanese saw these typhoons as divine interventions. They adopted the name Kamikaze for their WW II suicide pilots and their aircraft – in hopes that the American invasion fleet would be destroyed by their man-made Divine Wind.)

CHAPTER 10

THE LAST ISLAND – OKINAWA

We woke up the next morning after having spent most of the previous day and all night on the beach. I had stayed at the shell crater and was OK. My buddies who had spent the night in the shore caves were complaining of eye irritation. They had puffy eyes, and that was the end of their sleeping in caves. We never did find out what caused the irritations.

The first waves of ground force Marines had been told to expect an 80 to 85 percent casualty rate taking the beach. The invasion planners reached this figure because of the horrific casualties suffered during the invasions of Tarawa and Iwo Jima. But, the Marine infantry received only very small amounts of rifle and mortar fire during their approach in the landing craft. The beaches were deserted, and there was no enemy fire. The Marines were cautious as they walked upright onto the beaches. The calm was unreal, and everyone was asking the same question: Where are the Japs?

(We later learned that the Japanese battle plan required them to execute an advanced strategic withdrawal just before the invasion. Their plan was to cause the maximum number of casualties among the American forces – just like at Iwo Jima. Rather than risk casualties from American air strikes and naval artillery on the open ground on and just inland of the beaches, the Japanese would give the American infantry the beaches and airfields. Then, with their forces intact, they would wait for the U.S. Army and Marines to come to them. They would be waiting with intense crossfire from their heavily-armed caves in the southern ridges of Okinawa. And, at the same time, they would attack the offshore U.S. fleet with large numbers of Kamikaze aircraft.)

The U.S. invasion plan had allowed 3 days to take Kadena and Yontan airfields. But they were deserted and undefended also. The Marine infantry entered the abandoned airstrips unopposed by noon of the first day.

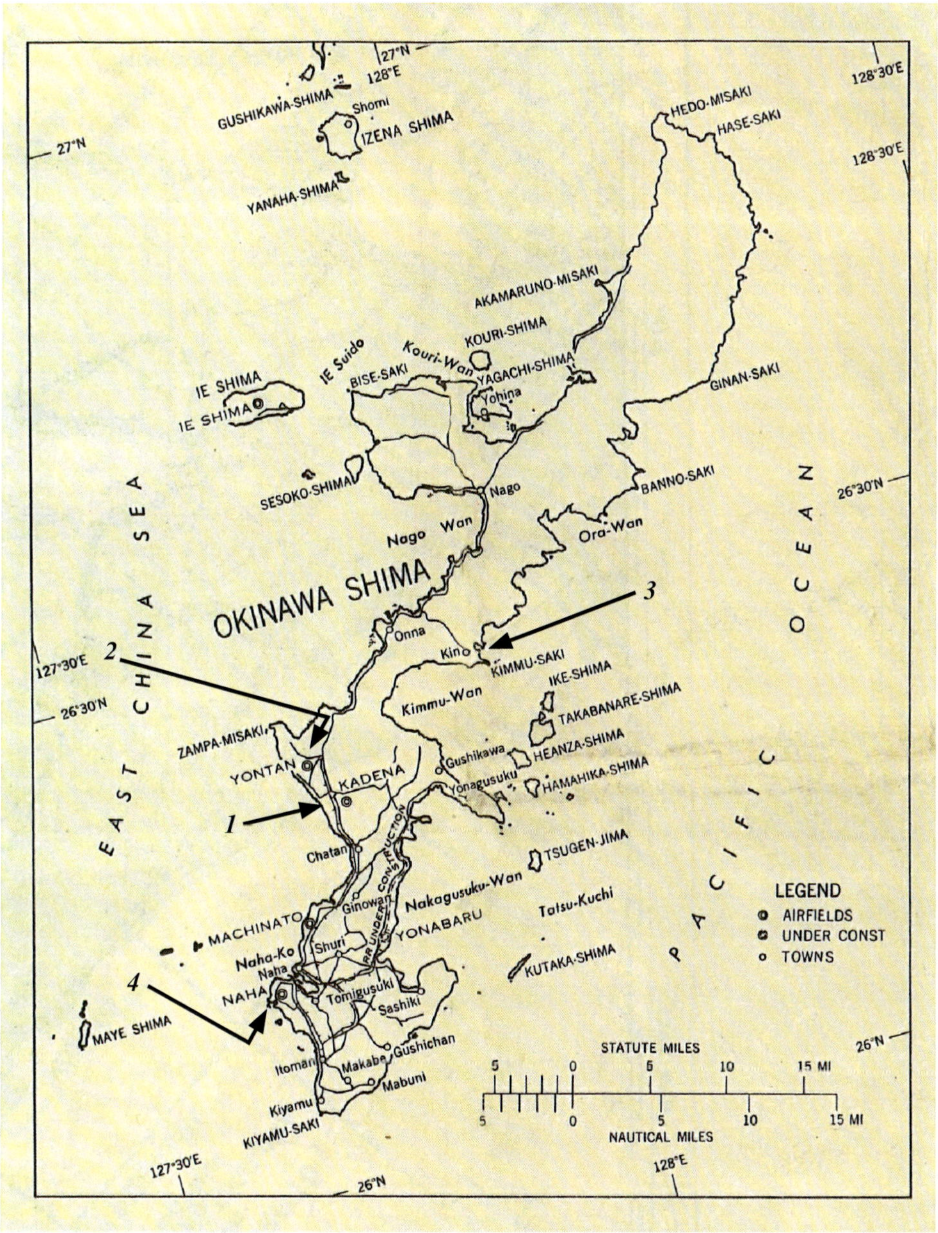

1. Kadena Airfield
2. Yontan Airfield (3 mi. from Kadena)
3. Town of Kin
4. City of Naha (capitol)

It was now the second day, and still there were no Marine officers around to give us orders. Because there were apparently no Japs remaining on the west side of the island where we were, we cautiously walked the 2 miles to Kadena airfield. We arrived there to find the airstrip deserted and in good condition. There were no bomb craters or booby traps. It didn't make sense to us. The airstrip could accept planes immediately.

The Navy medics came by and welcomed us to Okinawa by giving us shots for cholera and bubonic plague. Our left arms were numb and hung useless at our sides for a day. We couldn't lift anything – all we could do was walk around. We had to set up a tent compound to serve as our living quarters – something we had no experience doing. (The squadron tents at the established bases at Espiritu Santo and Ulithi were established before we arrived.)

We began struggling with the job of locating and setting up our tents. Fortunately, Lt. Fox, who was a 232 Avenger pilot, and Norm Tabaka, a 232 Technical Sergeant, came over from the officer's area to assist us. They had also come on the Freestone – probably to get an advance look at the condition of the airstrip. Officers usually didn't get involved with the day-to-day efforts of the enlisted men. But, they were veterans who had experience in camp set-ups from having been to the Solomons on 232's "second trip" to the Pacific Theater.

They were good organizers and showed us how to locate and erect the tents so that we would have good living and working arrangements. They stayed with us until we got the tents up. We all thought they were down-to-earth guys – and we greatly appreciated what they had done to help us "third trippers" get a foothold in our first combat location.

Almost immediately, we began to deal with another enemy. The whole island was infested with fleas! We were soon covered with them from head to toe. We had been given some little aerosol bombs that sprayed DDT powder, but they brought only temporary relief. Our hope each night was that we could get to sleep shortly after spraying ourselves with the DDT. But, they always reinvaded us by morning. You could feel them crawling up your back and through your hair.

(Several weeks later, some of our Avengers were fitted with pesticide tanks and spray gear. They sprayed the entire island with DDT and exterminated the fleas. The Japanese didn't shoot at our spray planes: The fleas were their enemy, too. We didn't have any problem with fleas after that.)

Supplies of 100 pound bombs and aviation fuel were quickly coming off the cargo ships and were being trucked to an ammo dump about a mile east of Kadena Airfield. We got the job of taking the bombs off the trucks and stacking them in the bomb dump. We were instructed to do this "very gently". They told us that if the bombs were dropped from the truck, one in a hundred might explode from the impact with the ground.

The unloading soon became tedious work. So, we began to kick the bombs off the truck. This speeded up the work, and the comic relief line everyone used while unloading was, "Maybe this is the one."

It was the usual case for us to make light of dangerous situations with a little gallows humor. When you're young, this seems to be the natural way of things. (In the back of our minds, we all knew that some of us would not make it home. But, it was better to be smart-ass crazy than gloomy.)

After all this unloading and stacking of the 100 pound bombs, we were ready to arm our Avengers. But, our planes were not due to be delivered until 22 April -- almost three weeks away.

In the meanwhile, the Navy gave us "a little work". Task Force 58 was offshore to assist with the invasion. The battleships and heavy cruisers were shelling the Japanese defenses concentrated at the south end of the island. But, the aircraft carrier Essex would remain offshore for 3 days. It launched its two squadrons of Navy Avengers to support our ground forces with bombing and strafing runs against Japanese positions. The battle line they attacked was to the south, not far from Kadena.

The Avengers from the Essex had been armed prior to launch, and they flew directly from the carrier to their first ground forces support mission. After they dropped their bombs on enemy targets, they did not return to the Essex. Instead, they landed at the Kadena airstrip. We rearmed and refueled them. The plan was to keep from depleting the fuel and bomb supplies onboard the Essex. Their supplies were needed for the pending attacks on the main islands of Japan. So, we used the bombs and aviation fuel we had stockpiled at Kadena for their immediate strike missions to support the ground forces on Okinawa.

Because the Essex was available to support our ground forces for only the first 3 days, we had to make those 3 days count. The Essex Avengers took off and returned to Kadena for another reloading every 15 or 20 minutes. (It took about half an hour to rearm a plane under normal conditions.) We worked at this pace for 3 days and nights, without rest, except for very short catnaps during the infrequent lulls. They just kept coming back -- and we kept rearming them around the clock.

When the 3 days were over, we were all dog tired. Our legs were swollen from our being on our feet day and night – lifting and loading bombs. But, we didn't have a choice – that's what we had to do. School was over: We were now in a combat zone – and under battlefield conditions. This was now our war, and we had to fight it as conditions demanded.

We used 100 pound bombs for most of the reloads. You had to develop a system – using technique and rhythm – like a weightlifter. You had to pick up the bomb, lift it to your waist, then to your shoulder, and then push it up into the shackles at the top of the bomb bay. Then, while you held the bomb in place, someone else would lock the shackles.

It's amazing how strong you get doing that under increased pressure. It got to the point where you lifted the bomb in one motion, and then held it and hooked it to the shackles by yourself. Our incentive was heightened by knowing that we were working to support Marine ground troops who were constantly under fire at the battle line. The two squadrons of Avengers from the Essex amounted to 48 planes -- and we kept them flying and fighting.

Luckily, there were no on-the-ground collisions with the continuous landing, rearming, refueling and take-offs during these operations. There were no protective revetments alongside the airstrip at which to service the planes at Kadena as there were at Ulithi. The services were done along the sides of the airstrip. The pilots kept from colliding with each other by keeping alert for the ground traffic during take-offs and landings.

One night during this 3 day, non-stop effort, I was arming an Avenger by flashlight at the upper end of the airstrip -- and all my buddies were working at the other end. A Jap infiltrator came to the airstrip perimeter and took 5 shots at us. I didn't have my rifle with me – it was stacked in a tripod with some others near to where my buddies were working. Suddenly, I could hear my boot camp instructor saying, "Your weapon is your friend: Don't ever be without it." I felt like I was naked.

I was going to get the 30 caliber machine gun out of the tail gunner's position on one of the Avengers. Then I realized that – in the dark -- I might hit our own people who were loading other planes along the airstrip.

So, I hit the ground. I learned later that everyone else had hit the ground also. We crawled to our rifles, but the sniper had disappeared into the darkness. Luckily, he hadn't hit anyone. That was our first experience of directed hostile fire. Welcome to Okinawa. The Japs are your neighbors!

The next attack came after the Essex Avengers had departed to go north with the task force. It came in daylight – and from the air. We were at our tents when someone yelled, "Jap plane!" Three Japanese planes came roaring over the airstrip. I was the last one out of our tent. I looked up, and saw this plane coming toward us -- flying about as high as a two story building. My first reaction was – what a shot! So I raised my M-1 to sight in on the engine. Then I saw his guns flashing. And, his bomb bay doors were open and fragmentation bombs were dropping out. I let fly some appropriate Marine-speak, and jumped into a foxhole next to the tent. Sgt. Roby had already taken cover in there. He said, "Are you hit?" I said, "Hell no, move over!"

When the attack was over, I saw that our tent was riddled with bullet and shrapnel holes.

About 15 guys from our Ordnance Group were hit during that attack. Willis Knight was hit in the neck, but he didn't feel it right away. When he lay down that night, his neck hurt. So, he went to the doctor—who pulled out 4 or 5 five small pieces of shrapnel from the back of his neck. One of the guys hit that day was in really bad shape from his wounds. They had to send him to a hospital ship.

On a lighter note, we had a guy in the ordnance group named John Gorski. (He was not the same Gorski that was our DI at Norman.) When the planes attacked, he was on the latrine. And, he got hit across the legs by several pieces of shrapnel. He wanted a purple heart – for being wounded in action. Major Feldmeier said, "No way – you should have been on the ground." Gorski said, "But sir, I was on the latrine." The Major said, "I don't care if you had to s__t yourself, you should have gotten yourself on the ground."

I felt a little sorry for Gorski: He had shrapnel in his legs and didn't get a purple heart – or any sympathy. But, he sat there watching this plane come in and didn't follow standing orders. But he recovered quickly, and he would provide us with several interesting future moments during our time on Okinawa.

I hadn't written home since I left San Diego. These casualties made me think that maybe it was time. So, I got out the little pad of stationery that the Red Cross had given us when we shipped out on the Sea Ray, and I wrote to my parents.

When my mother got the letter and saw the little Red Cross logo at the top of the page, she got all shook up. She thought I was in the hospital – recuperating from a battle wound. She wrote and asked what had happened to me. I wrote back to say that I hadn't been wounded, and that the little Red Cross was just a reminder of who had given us the stationery. (Whenever I wrote home after that, I cut the Red Cross off the top of the page.)

Our Avengers still hadn't arrived from Ulithi, but they brought some Marine Corsair fighter planes to us that needed to have the wing guns realigned. We would fasten ropes to the tail from the crane bar on the back of a bomb truck, and then lift until the plane was level. Then we inserted these little periscope-with-crosshair type devices into small gun inspection ports in the underside of the wings. These allowed us to look through the gun barrels, back-to-front, at a standing target about 200 yards down the airstrip. We didn't fire the guns, but we'd align them on these targets to give the pilots accurate lines of fire – and to prevent a badly misaligned gun from shooting holes in the leading edge of the wing. We did wing gun realignments on Marine Corsairs 2 or 3 times.

We would get other requests for out-of-the-ordinary jobs from time-to-time. The second trippers of 232 learned to fix almost everything during their previous tour in the Solomons. They often had to work without the availability of spare parts. They learned to make parts from stuff that was lying around in scrap heaps there. They gave the squadron the reputation of being able to do jobs that not every ordnance group could handle. They were a great "can-do" bunch of guys.

One night they sent O. L. Richardson and myself to protect some SeaBees who were operating road machinery to repair and enlarge the airstrip. They were being shot at by Japanese snipers hiding somewhere along the perimeter. The SeaBees were turning off the lights on their road graders and rollers every few minutes. Then, they would turn them on again and continue to work – until the snipers began to shoot again.

We took a position to try to locate the sniper, but it was so dark you couldn't see a thing. Then an air raid began. Our anti-aircraft guns went off in response to the air attack, and we wanted to get out of the way before the spent ack-ack shrapnel came raining down on us. (What goes up must come down, and the heavier shrapnel fragments could break bones or even kill you.)

So we crawled – feet first – into a large water drainage conduit that ran under the airstrip. We had just settled into the conduit and were looking up to watch the action above. We could see the tracer rounds from our anti-aircraft guns climbing into the night sky, and sometimes we could see airplanes.

Suddenly, O.L. jumps out of the conduit and starts shaking his right arm. I thought a Jap infiltrator had been hiding in the conduit and had stabbed him. I quickly climbed out and shouted, "Where is he?" Just then, a rat ran out of his right sleeve. It was one of those Okinawa wharf rats – and he was huge! O. L. said, "I ain't getting back in there." I said, "Neither am I: I'll take my chances out here."

(Those rats were as big as rabbits. One day I was on the airstrip, and this rat was sitting up on his hind legs. I shot him with my M-1. I couldn't find the pieces -- he just disintegrated. Of course, I had to be careful to aim down as I shot. The bullet from an M-I could travel for miles. You had to be careful that you weren't shooting in the direction of our guys.)

The Japs bombed and shelled the airstrips at Kadena and nearby Yontan almost every night during April. There were times when we had to find relief from the stresses of sudden air attacks and random artillery shelling. One day, the guys found a Japanese phonograph. And, there was a record of Betty Hutton singing "Ole Man Mose' Is Dead". Betty Hutton was a popular singer in the states, and she appeared with comedian Bob Hope on his touring USO variety shows. (Betty can still be seen on the late show starring in "Annie Get Your Gun" and "The Greatest Show on Earth".)

"Ole Man Mose Is Dead" was a hit back home, and the guys liked to sing along. The problem came at the words, "…he kicked the buck, buck, bucket." It didn't take long for the guys to change "buck, buck, bucket" into Marinespeak – and sing with even more enthusiasm. They sang with the record over and over. Finally, Major Feldmeier had enough – so he took the record and broke it. Then, the guys found a Japanese record. They played it over and over – and tried to sing along in Japanese. (The Major broke that record, too.)

I was in charge of arming the Major's Avenger. And, I would cut his hair. After I'd given the Major 4 haircuts, he peeled off $6 – which was a lot of money. (In those days a haircut was usually 50 cents.).

The Major wanted to set up a barber shop for me so that I could cut lots of guys. But, I said, "No, I'm an ordnance man. I'm not here to cut hair, I've got a job to do." The barbering was just a sideline for a few enlisted men who were my close friends – and a few officers. (I still wonder why I preached to the Major like that – telling him my job and all. It must have sounded strange – coming from an 18 year-old PFC in the ground crew to a Major who was an Annapolis graduate. What was I thinking? But, he was probably used to classless talk in battle zones.)

Our Avengers finally arrived as promised on 22 April. I went to look for Judy. I found Corporal Krueger with the other newly-arrived members of 232. The first thing I asked him was, "Hey Eli, where's my dog?" He looked at me and said, "I'm sorry, Frank, but she's somewhere on Iwo Jima."

He said that they had flown from Ulithi and landed on Iwo to refuel for the final leg to Okinawa. He let her out for a pit stop – and she ran away. He looked for her during a 3 day rain delay -- until it was time to take off for Okinawa.

Eli was very apologetic for having lost her. He said that Iwo was not secured as was reported in the press. It was still very active with small arms fire and artillery shelling from Japanese holdouts. Judy must have been frightened by the noise of the explosions. When the weather cleared and refueling had been completed, Krueger had no choice but to continue on to Okinawa without her.

I was deeply disappointed that Judy was lost – to me and to the squadron. It was just one of those things that happens in wartime. Plans don't always work out. I hope that she survived and was taken in as a pet by a group of Marines on Iwo.

As soon as our Avengers arrived, they began to fly 3 or 4 sorties a day. Most of the strikes were against the Japanese fortified caves in the ridges to the south around Shuri. The pilots had to fly right at the caves that housed the large artillery pieces -- then pull out and climb vertically to try to lob the bombs into the caves. This was a hazardous maneuver that took a lot of pilot skill – and guts.

I was a friend of a turret gunner named Vincent DePaul Kelly. He was a Pennsylvania boy from the Scranton area, and I regularly cut his hair. One day he came to me and asked me if I would cut the hair of his pilot – who was going home after one more mission. I said yes, and it turned out that his pilot was Lt. Fox! I was glad to see him – and to cut his hair. I felt that I was partially repaying him for the help he gave us in setting up our tents.

While I was cutting Lt. Fox, he talked at length about the coming flight being his 50th mission. That meant it would be his last: He was being rotated home. And, he was getting married as soon as he got back to his girl in California. He was a second tripper – having served in the Solomons -- and he was so happy that the war was finally over for him.

Lt. Fox, Vince Kelly, and an Army artillery spotter named Cashman then took off on what should have been a routine mission. They would fly low near the battle line so that Cashman could look over the line for Japanese artillery flashes from caves. He would then report their location to his own artillery unit – who would then try to place a shell into or close to the spotted cave.

But, there was always the danger of being accidentally hit by an in-flight artillery, tank, or mortar shell during this type of low-fly mission. As fate would have it, that's what happened to Lt. Fox's Avenger. An Army artillery captain saw the hit. The plane crashed on our side of the battle line. The artillery captain got to the wreckage site a few minutes after the crash – but found that there were no survivors. He said it was probably a shell from one of our own mortars that hit the plane.

I felt the loss deeply, and it brought tears. The artillery observer I didn't know, but Vince Kelly was a longtime friend in the ordnance group. And Lt. Fox had reached across the line between officers and enlisted men to help us get organized with our tents. I was glad to have known them both. War is bad enough, but the worst events are those that happen when your buddies are killed by friendly fire.

Fred Folino was another pilot in the squadron. Once when he was on night patrol, he was guided by the land-based radar crew to intercept a plane flying just offshore. He came up behind it – and saw that it was a Japanese reconnaissance plane. He gave it two bursts from his wing guns – but missed. The recon plane began to take evasive action. Folino went to fire again – but found that he had run out of ammunition. But, Folino had eight air-to-ground rockets – four under each wing. On a chance he might hit the recon plane, he fired two – and missed. He then fired two more – and downed it.

This was WW II, and these rockets had no automatic guidance systems to home in on the target. But Folino was a skilled flyer who was able to lead the target by eye and score the hit. This was the first known instance in aviation history where an enemy aircraft was shot down with air-to-ground rockets. Lt. Folino received a commendation for his action.

Whenever we armed the planes, we didn't see a pilot or a gunner around. They were worried that something might go wrong – and a bomb might go off during the loading. I remember one time when they gave us a new type of fuse to put in the bombs. It detonated the bomb at a preselected altitude – 100, 75, 50 feet – rather than on impact with the ground.

They liked to use them for bombing Japanese airfields – because the shrapnel cone would spread sideways farther and damage airplanes on the ground over a large area. But they stopped using them because they were too dangerous. If someone came home with one or more of these bombs still hung up in the bomb bay, they would explode at the pre-set altitude during the landing approach and destroy the plane and crew – and maybe other planes and fellow Marines on the ground.

Our buddy Gorski was not a low profile guy. He had an annoying habit of getting up in the morning and serenading us with this song – probably his own composition: "Wake up bright in the morning, with a great big smile, and a good, good morning, have breakfast in bed with your honey, on a day that's bright and sunny, you'll find Its all worthwhile, if you roll out of bed with a smile."

All the guys responded to this with, "Shut the hell up" – or worse. Needless to say, this attempt at a rebuff only encouraged Gorski to continue singing every morning.

One day, Lt. Winters – one of our pilots -- came up to me and said, "Renda, I want you to load a 1,000 pound bomb in my plane". I was surprised by his request, and I asked him, "What do you want a 1,000 pound bomb for?" He said, "I spotted this cave, and the Japs roll out this big gun on a railroad track. They fire it, and then pull it back into the cave – and no one can hit it. The Navy is trying to hit the cave from offshore, the Army and Marine artilleries are shooting at it from the battlefields, and nobody can get it. And I'm going to drop that bomb in that cave."

I wanted to say that probably all he needed was a 100 pounder – because the Japanese gun crew would have stacked artillery shells in the cave alongside the gun. A 100 pound shell would have set off the magazine in the cave. But, he insisted that he wanted a 1,000 pounder, so I gave him one. I fused it up, loaded it in the bomb bay, and he took off.

About 20 minutes later, he came back. After he had landed, I could see that the leading edges of the wings were all dented. And, there was mud all over the airplane. I said, "What happened?" He said, "I dropped that bomb right into that cave – and the whole side of the ridge blew up."

Well, the phone started ringing: The Navy's thanking us, the Army's thanking us – everyone is thanking us for knocking out that gun. But the plane was so badly damaged that they pushed it aside. I don't remember if they ever flew it again. They probably just stripped it for repair parts.

We had one pilot, Captain Snow, who was a very aloof kind of guy. He would never give us the time of day. One morning, he came back from a strike mission, and the first thing I did – as usual – was to look at the masking tape we put over the machine gun opening in the leading edge of each wing. If the tape had been blown away, the guns had fired. His one gun hadn't fired.

He was angry about this and had me climb up on the wing with him to look at the suspect gun. He said, "I want you to take this gun apart and see if you can put it together right."

I checked it over, and everything on the gun worked as it should -- with the plane on the ground at 100 degrees or hotter. So, recalling my machine shop experience, I said, "I think what's happening here is that when you get to altitude, the cold air is shrinking the jacket down on the barrel, and the barrel is stuck in place and can't return to pick up the next round. Let me replace this barrel with a new one."

He agreed to try this, so I got a new barrel and screwed it into the gun. He took off for the next bombing run, and when he got back and landed, I saw that the masking tape was blown off both guns. The new barrel had solved the problem. When he got out of the cockpit, he just walked right by me. He never said "good job", or "thank you" -- or even gave me a glance or a nod. Because I was able to solve the problem on the first attempt, I thought he should have recognized me somehow.

(But, that was the kind of guy he was. Captain Snow seemed to have no personality at all: He was just an all-business pilot. And that's the way our relationship remained. After WW II, he went on to fly in Korea and Viet Nam. Maybe his style was his way to survive.)

At Kadena airfield, there were times when we didn't get much cooked food. But, Okinawa was loaded with goats. Someone got the idea to roast one. So, this guy shot a goat – thinking it would provide some fresh meat as a change from K rations. But, it was a very old ram. They tried to roast it, but it smelled so bad and was so greasy that no one could eat it. They had to throw it away. Instead of picking out some tender ewe or kid, he had picked out this tough old goat – probably the oldest, toughest one on Okinawa.

There was a little goat that would hang around our outfit. We would bend over, and it would butt us in the behind. It would love to do this, and we got a lot of laughs out of it. I guess the entertainment he provided saved him from being next on the roasting spit. (This was further proof that we would often act a little crazy to take the edge off living in a combat zone.)

One day, Sgt. Roby, Tech. Sgt. Tabaka, "Kit" Carson, Charles Henneman and myself each caught a "free-ranging" chicken. (They were loose because so many farm buildings had been destroyed by the shelling – from both sides of the battle lines.) We tied each of them to a stake so that we could get an egg every morning. Everyone got an egg the first morning except Sgt. Roby. So, he held his chicken up, looked her in the eye and said, "Now look, if I don't get an egg tomorrow, I'm going to wring your neck, pluck your feathers, cook you, and eat you." The next morning, everybody got an egg except Sgt. Roby. So, he picked up the chicken, wrung its neck, and began to pluck its feathers. Then, he saw that the chicken had been wounded by a piece of shrapnel. And Sgt. Roby just sat there smiling, with his blue eyes twinkling. We didn't know what was going through his mind. I'm sure he was wondering why it was his bad luck to have the only wounded chicken in the bunch. Even the chickens on Okinawa were casualties.

A couple of days later, the Navy Shore Patrol came through our area and shot *all* our chickens! We asked them why they did that. They said that the chickens carried germs – and they had orders to shoot them. So much for our dreams of eggs for breakfast.

After the bad luck he had with his chicken, Sgt. Roby came up with a scheme to prevent his having to get up during an attack in the middle of the night to run for his foxhole. Inside the tent, he dug down in the ground about 3 feet and put his cot in the hole.

But, as they say, it's not nice to try to fool Mother Nature. When the rainy season began in late April, his foxhole filled up with water. I can still see him sitting there – smiling – with his blue eyes looking at the water in his foxhole. Again, we wondered what he was thinking. Why was his luck so bad? He had to fill his "indoor" foxhole with dirt and dig a new one – away from the tent.

One day the guys found a drum of Japanese alcohol. They said they were taking it to Dr. Armbruster to get it tested – to see if it was OK to drink. They knew that if it was wood alcohol, they could go blind from drinking it. Later, I saw them drinking it – so I presumed the Doc said it was all right.

We had the craziest outfit. We had guys who were "borrowing" newly-arrived

Jeeps. They'd steal a Jeep, put fake numbers on it, paint it, and then run it down a dusty road. The dust stuck to the wet paint, and "aged" the Jeep to make it look just as dirty as the older Jeeps that were around the airstrip. You couldn't tell that the Jeep had been repainted.

So, this one guy, PFC Joe DiMuccio, pulled up into our area with "his" new Jeep. We all took one look at the Jeep and then said, "Hi, General." And he looked at us and said, "What's this 'General' s__t ?" We pointed to the one-star General tag on the front of the Jeep. DiMuccio looked and said, "Oh my God -- get the paint!" They quickly put fake numbers over the star and drove it up and down the road so the tag looked as dirty as the rest of the Jeep. He didn't live that down. After all, who could be dumb enough to steal a Jeep having a General's star on it?

But, despite these examples of crazy behavior, the guys in 232 were all basically in the Marine mold. Still, in some ways, they were different from each other -- depending on the number of trips they had made to the Pacific Theater. I was on my first trip, and everything was new for me. The guys who were second trippers had gained experience in the Solomons. They had seen it all before – except for the dreaded Kamikazes. And they had the coolness that came with the "been there, done that" attitude. They could fix almost anything, and they were much in demand for their expertise with ordnance and general plane repairs.

Part of their job was to train us first trippers – to show us things that were not covered in the stateside ordnance schools. We were grateful to have them around. But a lot of those guys were a little nuts. Maybe because they were second trippers and it had affected their minds. They were cool and crazy. But, I think being a little crazy might have helped them to deal with the war.

And, we had one third trip ordnance man who didn't appear to do anything. He'd sit down and make out like he was fishing – flicking an imaginary fly rod. I thought he was a little off his mind. Maybe he just coasted until somebody came across some problem they had never seen before. (But, I never saw this happen. He must have worked behind the scenes. I learned later that he had some kind of responsibility for squadron safety – with a good record.)

One of the second trippers, Archie Page, had the name of every island he'd been to tattooed on his arms. He, too, was a little nuts. He may not have always known where he was going – but he always knew where he had been.

By now, the ground crews felt the bonds of being part of an air squadron that had mastered Marine teamwork in combat. Kadena and Yontan were under almost constant air attacks and artillery shelling by the Japs, and enduring these attacks strengthened this bond. I guess it was our version of the "Band of Brothers" effect.

I also felt a bond with the pilots. I loaded their bombs, and they delivered them to protect our ground forces. I guess I felt that all the guys, officers and enlisted men, were deliberately working hard together to defeat a vicious and suicidal enemy.

Al Andreucci was in our tent and one of the two field cooks for the squadron. For a while, we didn't have any cooked food – just K rations. One day they set up a mess tent, and someone said that we're going to have some real food cooked for us. So, we ran down to the mess tent, and there they gave each of us a pancake about the size of a silver dollar. And I said to Andreucci, "Is this all we get?" And he said, "That's all there is." So, we each ate our tiny pancake. They didn't even have any syrup. All they had were those little packs of jelly like you get in a diner. So we put that on the pancake, and in one bite, it was gone.

As we were eating our pancakes, we saw two Japs sneaking down the hill toward us. I guess they were going to hit us while we were at chow. Or, maybe they were hungry because they were cut off from their food supplies and intended to steal some of our food when they saw an opportunity.

Someone saw them and yelled. Everyone grabbed his rifle. And when the Japs saw that our guys had spotted them, they turned around and ran back up the hill. The hill was honeycombed with caves – and they ran into one of them. We saw which cave it was, and some of the guys wanted to build a fire and smoke them out.

The fire was lit, and we were lying in front of the cave with our rifles ready. But then we saw the smoke coming out on the other side of the hill! It was typical for the Japs to lengthen the caves through the hills to make tunnels. They had escaped out the other end – and we never did get them.

All the privates and PFCs had guard duty. The corporals didn't have to do it. Every other night, we had to guard the perimeter of our outfit at the airstrip. The night before I first began guard duty, one of our guys shot a Japanese infiltrator who was creeping toward our tents. I asked him what happened, and he said, "This Jap was coming toward me – so I shot him." And, he used a Thomson sub-machine gun for a "can't miss" advantage. I said, "Did you yell Halt! 3 times like it says in the guard manual?" He said, "Not when he started speaking Japanese."

I looked at the body of the infiltrator the next day, and something about it puzzled me. The guy was not wearing a uniform: He was wearing civilian clothes. And, I noticed that his haircut was that of an officer. Why would a Japanese (or Okinawan conscript) officer try to sneak into our area wearing civilian clothes – and respond to the guard's command to halt by speaking in Japanese? Was this guy trying to surrender? That wasn't likely because of the Japanese military code. Was he a spy or an assassin? I guess I'll never know.

There were a couple of 232 pilots who were also looking at him while I was there, but I didn't know them. So, we didn't exchange guesses about this Japanese infiltrator.

The next night I had guard duty at that same post. You're supposed to lay still on the ground so you don't show a silhouette. And, your imagination makes you think that everything is moving. And I kept repeating to myself, "Not until you see the whites of their eyes." You don't want to give away your position. You had to lay still for the entire four hour shift – until you got relieved.

Then one night they moved me to a different post. The guard I took over from said, "Renda, stay behind this boulder. There's a Jap out there who's been sniping at me all night." I said, "Don't worry, I will." But I guess the sniper saw the Jeep pull up to drop me off, and he must have figured they were bringing up several guys as reinforcements. I don't know where the sniper went, but I wasn't bothered during my entire shift.

The next morning we went up to look for the sniper's nest. We found a foxhole dug in some clay-type soil. The sides of it were so smooth they looked like they had been cut with a knife. The floor was smooth, too. It was like a box. It was a typical Japanese excavation – precision work.

Guard duty had a basic drawback. You had to do it every other night, and you couldn't sleep the next day because you had your other regular duties. Again, the only guys who got this guard duty were the privates and the PFCs: We were the low men on the totem pole.

We had another food disaster at the mess tent. Someone said that we had "fresh meat". So, after a steady diet of K rations for several weeks, I thought I'd go to see what they had. I went down to the mess tent and saw these sides of beef hanging there. From a distance, they looked white. As I got closer, I saw that the beef sides looked like they were moving. They were covered with maggots! The cooks had buckets of water and were washing the maggots off the beef.

They cut up the beef and cooked it. At chow time, when it came time for me to get my piece of beef, I said I didn't want any. A buddy looked at me and said, "What's the matter with it?" I said, "Nothing, I just don't want any." They asked me if I was sick. I repeated that I just didn't want any. Instead, I ate some of the dehydrated vegetables. What I didn't say was that on one of the few times I was out in the field, I saw dead Japanese covered with maggots. That was reason enough for me to decide I wouldn't eat that beef.

On a brighter side of mess tent experiences, there was Tech Sgt. Tabaka's coffee. Norm Tabaka was a good friend of mine, and he was an Ordnance man. (With Lt. Fox, he helped us set up our tents.) He would make coffee for us some mornings.

He was a friend of a guy in the mess tent, and this guy would loan him one of those gasoline burners that you pumped – like a camp stove.

So, on those mornings when it was convenient for everyone, Norm would get a big pot of water – and a pound of coffee from the mess hall. He would bring the water to a boil, and pour the pound of coffee into this big pot. When it got to be the right color, he took a canteen of cool water and slowly dribbled it around on the surface of the coffee. The cold water would bring the grounds down to the bottom of the pot. Then he'd ladle the coffee into our cups. It tasted wonderful – probably because it was cooked fresh in a place where almost everything else we got to eat or drink was pre-cooked and packed 8,000 miles away – and took months to reach us.

I also remember the first movie we saw on Okinawa. They had set up a movie screen, and we sat on the side of a hill facing it. The movie was "The Horn Blows at Midnight", starring comedian Jack Benny. So, we're sitting there enjoying the movie, and we suddenly hear the sound of a Japanese plane in a dive. He must have been either on a night patrol or a heckle flight and had seen the movie screen. I'm sure this made him want to strafe the hillside and kill all the Marines in that open air theater. We all got up and ran for our lives down the hill to get away from his target area.

We got out of the way just in time, but one of my buddies, Leno Sacco, tripped and fell. Still running at full speed, the rest of us just stampeded right over him. He finally got up, and I'm laughing at him. He was angry and said, "What are you laughing at?" We had just escaped strafing and were unharmed. I was glad for it – but saw some after-the-fact humor in his trampling. So I said, "It looked so funny." He said, "I don't think it was funny."

We continued on to our bomb trucks – and got under them in case some shrapnel from our own anti-aircraft shells would fall down on us. But Leno was still upset that we had laughed at him – and I don't think he ever got over it.

Leno was an Italian boy from the Chicago area, and I remember a time he got a package from home. It was a sausage – a pepperoni. And, it was all moldy. (It took a month for a package to reach us from the states.) He was going to throw it away. I said, "Don't throw that away." He said, "I ain't eating that pepperoni." I said, "I'll eat it." So, I wiped the mold off it – and it was good. All the mold was on the outside of the casing, the inside was fine. (There's a difference between sides of beef with maggots and a sausage made with preservatives inside a protective casing.)

Sometimes, when the target zone was close by, we would load the bombs into our Avengers and then drive as close as we could to the front lines to watch our pilots in action. One day, several of us – L.E. Bowers, Bill Murphy, Gus

Perilli, Don Neild and myself -- took a bomb truck down the Naha road towards the front lines. We had to stop to get our bearings. Bowers had a box camera and wanted to take our picture. Perilli, Neild, and myself stood in front of a stone wall and posed –- partly because we wanted to show the unusual way the Okinawans aligned the stones to build the wall. The stones are set on the diagonal and wedged into each other – perhaps to keep the walls from collapsing during earthquakes.

After Bowers took the picture, we got back on the truck and continued to drive south. We saw some Marine infantry dug in to the right side of the road – and they were looking at us oddly. A tank was somewhere nearby and was shooting a round off now and then.

We saw a town ahead – about a city block away – and drove towards it. But we had to stop because there was a bomb crater in the road. We couldn't get by it because there were deep gullies on both sides of the road. The crater was filled with muddy water from a recent rain – and we couldn't tell how deep it was by looking. So, we got out to walk to the town to check it for souvenirs.

As we were getting off the truck, we noticed there was a barbed wire fence there – and quite a few dead Japs lying to the other side of it. We were curious as to what killed them, so we jumped over the barbed wire fence and walked around to take a closer look. Bill Murphy and Lloyd Bowers kept walking down the road towards the town – probably to get first crack at souvenirs.

They hadn't gone very far when the Marine sergeant started yelling at us and waving us back. Murphy kept walking towards the town, but the rest of us walked back towards the Marine sergeant to see what he wanted. Then he said, "Where the hell do you guys think you're going?"

We said we were going to the front lines. He said, "You're already past the front lines -- and we've been trying to take that town for two days! And, in case you didn't notice, you've just walked through a mine field!"

Then we heard rifle fire coming from the town, and we saw Murphy running towards us. When he got back to us, we asked Murphy if he was the one who was shooting. He said, "Yes, the place is crawling with Japs!" We all got back into the truck and got out of there. All the while we were there the dug-in Marines looked at us as though we were nut cases. They were right.

That was the last time I tried to go to the front lines. The unclear locations of mine fields had made me wary of the dangers. I wasn't experienced in walking through mine fields, and I wanted to be able to walk on my own legs when I got home. I would be satisfied to continue to take my chances with Japanese artillery shells, air attacks and knife-wielding infiltrators at the airstrip.

But, we did other crazy things. We were all young – 18 or 19 years old. We went anywhere – we would just take off when we would have some break time. I used to go to the town of Kin. It was north of Kadena -- away from the big battlegrounds in the south. There were civilians there – both the townspeople and an ever-increasing number of refugees from the south. Out of curiosity, we'd go there to walk around and mingle with these people – just to get an idea as to what they were like.

There were ethnic Chinese, ethnic Japanese, and native Okinawans in the town. The Okinawans were a mix of Chinese, from the earliest immigrations, Japanese, from the more recent immigrations -- plus a little Malayan from the earliest settlers. The Japanese ruled the island and didn't like the Chinese. They had been at war with the Chinese since invading mainland China in the mid 1930's. And they didn't like the Okinawans, who they saw as an undesirable mixed breed of Chinese and Japanese.

The Okinawans knew that the Japs looked down on them -- and they resented it. After all, the Okinawans – even though they were a multiethnic mix -- were the native people that had been forced to live first under Chinese and then Japanese rule over the years.

The Japanese had committed war atrocities against Chinese civilians on the mainland during the late 1930's and early 1940's. The fact that we were liberating Okinawa from the Japanese made us heroes to the local ethnic Chinese. Many Okinawan civilians had been conscripted by the Japanese and were forced to fight us. They had a "must" loyalty to the Japanese: The Japanese paid their wages. Other Okinawans were conscripted to do construction work – building defensive fortifications for the Japanese. We weren't sure what they thought of us.

Most of the non-conscripted Okinawan civilians were friendly -- and treated us like liberators. For our part, we treated the Chinese and Okinawans with respect – and provided them with food and medical services. Most of the population on Okinawa lived in the south. That's where the intense fighting was taking place. They suffered collateral damage both from us and the Japanese. Many of the refugees who were old or wounded and half-starved were walking north to seek safety. We would pick up these terrified people from where they had collapsed along the roads – and trucked them to the battle-free areas farther north. There we would give them food, medicine and protection.

I remember there was this one resident Chinese family in Kin, and they were very glad to see us. They had been under the heel of the Japanese for a long time, and they were glad for our arrival. They saw us as heroes and liberators. The father liked to walk around with us – strutted is a better word. He had been a second class citizen his whole life, and now he was with the victors. (Most people don't know we were WW II allies with the mainland Chinese in the fight against the Japanese.)

We brought this Chinese family food. We also brought them a ewe and a nanny goat – so they could have milk for their small children. One time, the wife cooked a rice dish for us in appreciation for our help. It was freshly cooked and very tasty. We really enjoyed it.

Kin is in an area called Ishikawa – which is very beautiful. There is a valley with farms and rice paddies just south of the town. Fortunately, there were no air raids or ground battles there, so this area was not devastated by the war. We would go there once in a while, a few of us, just to walk around and enjoy the pastoral beauty of the place.

On one of our excursions, we went to an area north of Kin. There were some Army guys sitting on a log along the side of the road. They all appeared to be in their late twenties – ancients compared to us 18 and 19 year old Marines. They looked at us and said – in an unfriendly tone of voice -- "What are you *kids* doing here?"

We bristled and said, "What do you mean, '*kids*'?" By this time we considered ourselves veterans, and it sounded like we were being challenged and insulted. So they quickly said, "Hey, no offense, no offense." I remember that they were in the 27th Army Division. We always had a little inter-service rivalry with both the Army and the Navy. But, the moment passed and we kept going. My best memory of this encounter was that we were so young, and these guys seemed so old. On looking back, they were just kidding us, but we didn't get it at the time.

A bit farther up the road we saw a "Kilroy was here" sign posted in a wooded area. We think the guys from the 27th put it up. This sign was of a WW II icon – a cartoon of a little guy peering over a board fence. It was rumored to be the additional signature of an inspector in a stateside aircraft plant. He would mark a part within specs, "OK, passed" -- and then add this little cartoon sketch on the parts he had inspected and approved. It caught on as a way to show that U.S. armed forces had already "been there" to whoever came into an area afterwards.

On another visit to an area north of Kin, I was souvenir hunting with my buddy, Bill Ashley. We were getting ready to leave when we noticed a group of SeaBees with rifles on some high ground. They had made a barricade of what looked like big equipment boxes. While we were looking at this arrangement, one SeaBee walked over to me and said, "Hi, Frank." Here, it was Frank Sciortino – from York! We couldn't believe we met in this remote part of a Pacific island. This was a "small world, isn't it" meeting if ever there was one.

He told me that there were still Japanese in the area. They hid during the daylight hours. But, every night at dusk, they would storm out of the surrounding hills and charge at the SeaBees -- yelling and shooting.

The SeaBees would return fire from the barricade of boxes. He asked if we would stay with them overnight to help defend their group. Also, he was concerned that we would be taking to the road this late in the day – with Japs in the area. Then came one of those times when you have to make a tough decision. Here's a hometown buddy with a request for help – and a concern for our safety. But, Bill and I had a duty to get back to base to service our planes.

I told him that we couldn't stay – we had to get back. We didn't have a vehicle, so we just started hitchhiking down the road. Luckily, some guy in a Jeep happened by and picked us up. He was alone and looking for company – and he was heading south. So, we got a ride to Kadena just as our break time was over. (Frank Sciortino and his fellow SeaBees made it through OK.)

We also provided work for some civilian Okinawans. We set up a laundry near our tent. And these young Okinawan women would do our laundry – using a washing machine we somehow got from the Navy. They charged us 10 Yen – which was about 10 cents – to wash our clothes.

And they wanted to know what their names were in English. So, the guys made up different names that were inside jokes. One woman was called "Ipana" – because she had no front teeth. (The Ipana toothpaste ads claimed that it gave one "The smile of beauty.")

Another woman was called "Mabel" from the old bar joke, "Get off the table, Mabel – the dollar's for the drinks." All of these laundry women were given gag names. And they were proud of their new English names – whatever they were.

All day long they worked, and as they worked they sang the same song -- over and over. We guessed the title was something like, "Okinawa, the Beautiful Island". We would try to sing along – and eventually we learned the words. The girls got a kick out of our attempts to sing in Okinawan. (After 70 years, I still remember all the words and can sing the song.)

There were three communal bathing pools at Kin, arranged in 3 tiers. The water flowed from the upper tier to the middle tier to the bottom tier. The men bathed in the upper tier, and the women bathed in the middle tier. The young girls bathed in the bottom tier. The boys bathed in a creek nearby. (On some days, the upper tier was used for sponge bathing and clothes washing.)

There was a rail alongside the third tier, and we would rest our elbows on it to watch the girls bathing. They didn't like us to be watching them, and they would splash us to try to move us along. (That was the slowest we ever moved on

Okinawa.)

Once they sent me to guard 10 Japanese prisoners on a work detail. They were among the few Japanese that had allowed themselves to be captured – rather than commit suicide. (They knew they could never go home: The stigma of surrender rather than to die for the Emperor would make them outcasts forever in Japan.)

They had been set to work at a large tent – digging drainage ditches under the floorboards. We were getting a lot of rain, and they wanted to make sure the runoff water would drain away and not flood the tent.

One of the prisoners spoke very good English, and he asked me, "Is it true that to be a U.S. Marine you have to kill your mother and father?"

I looked him in the eye and slowly answered him with, "That's right, we did." I put this in Marine speak for emphasis, and that was the end of the conversation. This was a deliberate lie: I wanted the prisoners to be afraid of me.

(This was typical of the lies that Japanese officers would tell their enlisted men to raise their level of hatred against the Marines. The Japanese rank and file deeply respected their parents, and this propaganda was very effective in convincing them that all Marines were ruthless barbarians. It also further discouraged any desire to surrender to the Americans.)

One of the prisoners in this group was about 6 feet tall. This was unusual for a Japanese. So I asked the English-speaker, "How come he's so big and tall – compared to the rest of you guys?" And the guy said, "He's from the north island of Hokkaido – where the Japanese are bigger." Whether that's true or not, that's what he told me.

Well, this big Jap told the guy who could speak English that he wanted to go back to where he had been working before the tent detail to get his jacket. I didn't like the look on his face when the English speaker translated this request to me, but I said, "OK, go get it." I had a .45 pistol, and when he started to walk away he turned around and saw me with my hand on the .45. Then he came back and said he remembered that he didn't have a jacket that day after all.

A Marine Major close by had seen and heard this exchange. He came over to me and said, "I don't want you to talk to any of these guys. If they give you any crap, just shoot 'em."

On another guard duty, I had to take a prisoner from the brig to the chow line. He must have been in for some relatively minor infraction because he was allowed to go there every other day. His brig mate was Rice – the artist that had stolen the high-powered binoculars on board the Freestone. But Rice could have a chow line meal only every third day. The other two days he got only "Piss and Punk" – bread and water.

When I'd arrive to take the other guy to chow, Rice would say, "Please, Frank, bring me back some food." I felt sorry for Rice, and as I was walking his brig mate to chow, I told him, "Look, when I take you to the chow hall to get your food, I'm going to turn my head – and you can put some food in your pocket to take back to Rice."

So, that's what we did. I know I could have gotten into trouble, but I felt sorry for Rice. He thanked me so much for allowing him to get a little extra food. I lost track of Rice after my brig guard duty was over. The guy was a terrific artist – he could really draw and sketch. It was a sad waste of talent that he got himself into big trouble like he did. But, it was his own fault – and stupid.

The spring rains came at the end of April and would continue for most of May. They were especially heavy in 1945, and the roads turned into two feet of sticky mud with deep pools of water at the low spots. The supply trucks would get stuck in the mud and couldn't get through to the front lines with their cargo of food, water, medicine, grenades, and ammo. Then they tried to carry these supplies with tanks, but they bogged down too. They even tried Amtracs (Amphibious tanks) – but they would become stuck in the gooey mud also.

With the trucks unable to get through, the front line infantry troops would find themselves running out of these essential supplies. They would have to stop fighting – and sometimes give back ground. The plan was to set up airdrops to deliver these supplies. The airstrips were wet, but they were in better shape than the roads. The Avengers would set up a spray curtain as they took off – but they could fly to the battle lines as airborne delivery trucks.

Parachute packs were a new type of bomb bay load for us in the Ordnance Group. They were packed with the required mix of supplies by the Air Delivery Section -- a Marine Group that specialized in preparing parachute packs that could be air-dropped. Several of the Air Delivery Group came to Kadena and showed us how to hang these parachute packs on the shackles in the bomb bays of the Avengers. And, they took movies of us hanging them. I got into one of these film takes – just to show that ordnance guys could learn the technique. These films were then used for training ordnance guys at other airfields.

An airdrop mission requires different flight tactics from a strike mission. The frontline Marine infantry must put marker panels or smoke grenades on the ground to mark the target drop zone. The drop zone is typically a square -- only 150 feet on each side. The Avenger must be flown level and low – at about 150–200 feet in altitude. And it must fly slowly, at 100–120 mph. This slow speed allows the parachute packs to be dropped without ripping the chutes when they pop open, and prevents them from hanging up in the bomb bay. (It also makes the Avenger a more vulnerable target.)

If the pilot drops the parachute packs too soon, the infantry guys would have to walk back to retrieve them, and then carry them a long distance through the mud to get back to the battle line. This might cost them some ground, and they would then have to retake it. If the pilot drops the parachute packs too late, they will fall into enemy territory, and the Japs will recover the parachute packs. The food, water, grenades and medical supplies were welcomed by the Japs: They had battlefield shortages also.

The success rate for 232's Avengers hitting the drop zones was in excess of 97%. These flights saved the ground troops from running out of key supplies. And, they did not have to retreat from hard-won ground to pick up parachute packs that were dropped too soon. Our Avengers brought the desperately needed supplies directly to the front. The ground forces could hold on -- and keep advancing.

This on-the-spot delivery was not an easy mission. The pilots approached the drop zones by flying directly towards the battle line. The final approach required steady nerves – and guts. Only after he has released the parachute packs at just the right moment to hit within the drop zone can the pilot turn for home. Only a few seconds after the drop, he would cross the battle line and be over enemy territory. He would now be targeted from dead ahead and from both sides with ack–ack and all manner of small arms fire. The pilot must quickly do a 180 to get back to the friendly side of the battle line.

One day I asked Lt. Godbold if I could fly with him as a gunner on one of these airdrop flights. He knew I could handle the Avenger's guns, and he said yes. He let me take the turret gun. This is a .50 caliber twin machine gun, and you sit facing the tail to protect the plane against enemy aircraft attacking from the rear. The tail gunner / radio operator for this mission was a guy named Fred Carter. His station was on the underside of the plane – also facing rearward.

At this time, there were fewer Japanese fighter planes active over Okinawa. There would be a few now and then, but our combat patrols would shoot most of them down before they could get to us. This improved the odds for our not coming under attack from the air. We suspected that most of the Japanese pilots now coming to Okinawa were inexperienced: The best Japanese pilots were now kept in the home islands to defend key targets against American bomber attacks.

I didn't have to fly this mission, but I knew Lt. Godbold. I had a great deal of respect for his flying skills. So, I dared myself to do it – and up I went.
Lt. Godbold put the parachute packs right into the drop zone, and the flight seemed to me to be going OK. Then the tail began bouncing up and down. Lt. Godbold called me on the intercom and said, "Renda, do you see anything back

there?" I said, "Well, there are some puffs of black smoke behind the plane." He said, "That's ack-ack." I hadn't heard any noise because of the roar of the Avenger's 1,900 horsepower engine. We must have just crossed the battle line, and the concussions from the exploding Japanese ack-ack shells were lifting the tail.

Lt. Godbold turned the Avenger hard to the left to take us north. He got us out of there in a hurry, and we headed back to Kadena. I glanced down at Fred Carter. He was flattened out on the piece of armor plate that shields him from ack-ack shrapnel and small arms fire from below. I was on top of the plane and couldn't see the ack-ack coming up. He was on the bottom of the plane – and had a bird's eye view of any ground fire that was coming at us.

On the way back I started to think about what I would do if we got hit. We were too close to the ground to bail out – our chutes wouldn't open in time. I'd have to stay with the airplane. Luckily, there were no hits. After we landed, Lt. Godbold asked me if I was ready to go again. I said something like, "No, not just yet." He laughed. And that was my only time on a parachute drop mission. It was a thrill, and one that has lasted a lifetime.

It was ironic that an aircraft originally designed to attack enemy ships with torpedoes would end up hauling supplies to come to the rescue of ground forces. Someone deserves the credit for how versatile the Avengers – and their pilots – turned out to be. During those critical and muddy weeks in May and the first week in June, they came through by providing the immediate and most urgent resupplies to the Marine Infantry in the largest, longest, and highest casualty battle of WW II.

The Avenger squadrons were officially recognized for the airdrop supply missions they flew. The advances of the ground war would have been halted by the mud for weeks -- had it not been for VMTB – 232 –- together with our companion Avenger squadron, VMTB – 131.

For all the good service the Avengers provided for the ground forces, they were popularly known in the field as "Turkeys" -- a seemingly negative nickname. When airborne, the protruding rear gunner/radioman's compartment on the underside of the plane made it look awkward. When parked on the airstrip, the tall landing gear contributed to their comic appearance. Avengers did not have the lethal look of the Corsair fighters, but they were effective and tough.

When men on the ground would see Avengers coming to resupply them, they'd cheer, "Here come the Turkeys." The pilots swore by their stable behavior in flight, and their life-saving deliveries of much-needed supplies made them heroic to the ground troops. And, as with other planes made by Grumman, they could take a lot of battle damage and keep flying.

One final comment: Some Japanese aviation brass said they thought the Corsairs were overrated (sour grapes), but they regretfully respected the Avenger for its capabilities.

At Kadena airfield, one of the guys in our tent was Lee "Kit" Carson. He always said that he was related to the real Kit Carson. We all said, "Yeah, sure." And Kit was always saying that he didn't believe in God. He'd say, "That's a bunch of baloney. The only reason they have religion is so people don't kill each other."

And then one night we really got shelled. The next morning, he got out of his foxhole and said, "Gather round, boys, gather round. I want to tell you something. I don't know who I was praying to last night – but I was praying." And he never talked about God after that. I guess foxhole conversions can happen at unexpected times -- and to unexpected people.

To protect ourselves against Japanese infiltrators sneaking into our tent, we always kept one round out of the chamber of our M-1 rifles. We did this so we didn't have to lose time trying to work the safety – which is small and difficult to find and release in the dark. Instead, to load the first shot, we would throw the bolt back: It was quicker to work than the safety, and that would put one round into the chamber – and you were ready to shoot.

At 2 a.m. one night, I'm on my cot, and I heard the tent flap sliding open. I saw someone creeping into our tent. I threw my bolt back – and 7 other bolts were immediately thrown back also. The intruder said, "Don't shoot – it's me, Wallace." (Yes, he was the same guy who tried to wrestle me down at Santa Barbara.) We said, what the hell are you doing -- coming in here in the middle of the night? We were well aware of guys getting their throats cut by Japanese infiltrators – who would slip into the tents under cover of darkness.

Wallace said, "I have guard duty tonight, and I want to borrow Henneman's Thomson submachine gun." Coming from Wallace, this was taken by everyone as a "likely story". We were always on alert in case someone would try to steal it. At this point, "Kit" Carson said, "Get out, and don't you come in here again, day or night without letting us know ahead of time. Better yet, just don't come in here – ever again."

On the night of 29 April, they shelled Kadena again. My foxhole was full of water. After the first two shells had come in, I jumped into a foxhole with two of my buddies, O.L. Richardson and Donald Neild. O.L. was complaining, "There's not enough room in here for three guys." Donald replied, "Well, what's he supposed to do?" So, they let me stay. I said two "Hail, Mary's", closed my eyes, and fell asleep.

That night they delivered 28 artillery shells on us – and they were big ones. I heard the first 2, but I slept through the next 26. They were shelling right along the airstrip – which is where our tents and foxholes were. The shells were spaced out time-wise. This was a common practice. Their main objectives were to destroy our planes and kill and wound Marines. The shelling would also disrupt our sleep all night and make us fatigued the next day.

In the morning, the shelling was over. O.L. and Donald were out of the foxhole and telling everyone from the other foxholes that I had slept through the night. They all wondered how I could have slept through this artillery barrage – and emerged full of vim and vigor. Had I been hit? No such luck. They had been kept awake through the shelling and were standing around with bloodshot eyes. They were complaining because I had gotten a night's sleep – and they hadn't.

The rains continued through most of May. We got so much rain that we were almost up to our knees in mud or water. When you walked in it, you'd have to pull your legs up – there was such a suction. It made getting around very difficult – and slow. We wore a boot shaped like a work shoe. You sometimes left the shoe behind when you walked in that mud; then you had to dig it up and clean it out.

One time Gorski took 4 guys for a ride in one of our Jeeps. They got lost close to the front lines and decided to turn back. He pulled into a clearing to turn around – and there was a group of Japanese troops there! They were lined up and standing at attention. Gorski drove slowly around the lineup – hoping to exit the clearing without a fight. The guys in the Jeep were looking at the Japs, and the Japs were looking at the guys in the Jeep. No one called out or moved, and no shots were fired. Gorski exited the clearing and made for the base. (Maybe the Japs wouldn't act without orders – or maybe they thought the war was over.)

They began to bring bigger planes to Kadena because the airstrip was long enough to handle the long-range heavy bombers that were now beginning to attack the home islands of Japan. So, they moved our Avengers to Awase Airfield – which was nearby. It had a shorter airstrip – but it was long enough for Avengers.

On 10 May, Lt. Klingman was on patrol from Kadena in a four Corsair division as wingman to Captain Ken Reusser. They happened across a Japanese photo reconnaissance plane. It was flying at high altitude – probably to take photos to guide their Kamikaze pilots to key targets on land and in the fleet. Reusser and Klingman dumped some fuel and shot some ammunition to lighten their Corsairs so they could climb to the higher altitude of the recon plane.

As they approached the enemy recon plane, they saw that it was a Kawasaki "Nick" twin engine fighter-bomber. It had a rear-facing machine gun in the rear part of the crew cabin. Captain Reusser fired on the Nick. It took some hits, but began to climb. Lt. Klingman's Corsair had better performance and continued to climb in pursuit of the Nick – firing a few rounds on the way in the cold air at 30,000 feet. But as they approached 36,000 feet, his guns froze in the cold air.

Lt. Klingman eased up behind the Nick with the intention of disabling the Nick's tail by clipping it with his propeller. The rear gunner in the Nick was trying to shoot at him – but his gun was frozen also. As the rear gunner was banging on his guns trying to free them, Lt. Klingman moved in and began to chew away the tail surfaces of the Nick with his propeller. The prop wash from the twin-engined Nick made it difficult for Lt. Klingman to hold his line of approach to the tail. He had to gain some altitude, then weave back and forth behind the Nick as he repeatedly dropped down to engage its rudder and horizontal stabilizers with his prop. After several minutes of this strange air combat, Klingman managed to cut off the Nick's tail surfaces. The pilot lost control, and the Nick fell and crashed into the sea.

After downing the Nick, Lt. Klingman saw that he was low on fuel. He didn't think he could make it to Kadena, so he made for Awase – which was closer. But he ran out of fuel on the way. We were there servicing our Avengers at the time, and we saw this Corsair approaching the airstrip. It wasn't making a sound. That surprised us because we weren't used to seeing no-power landings. He glided in and made a perfect dead stick landing – coming to a stop on the runway. A small group of us ran out and pushed his Corsair to the side of the airstrip – to make room for any other planes that might be coming in.

We talked to him when he was out of the cockpit and asked him what happened. He told us about the encounter. The tips of his prop blades had been curled over from the repeated contact with the tail structure of the Nick. Photographs of Lt. Klingman standing beside his damaged propeller tips were widely published at the time. He was 28 when this happened – 5 or 6 years older than the average fighter pilot. I remember him as a really nice guy. He was awarded the Navy Cross for downing the Nick under unusual and hazardous circumstances.

On the night of May 24 – 25, the Japanese attempted to land several air transports at Yontan airfield – only 3 miles north of Kadena. These planes carried Kamikaze commandos – armed with demolition charges, grenades, and submachine guns. They were to be deliberately crash-landed -- to halt their planes on the airstrip in the shortest amount of time. The objective was to get the commandos out of the transports and among our parked planes quickly. (Because it was a suicide mission, there were no arrangements to recover the commandos after the raid.)

As we learned later, the Japanese had planned to land 8 Kamikaze commando planes at Yontan and 4 at Kadena during the same attack. Each of these planes carried 14 commandos. Lucky for us, 4 had to turn back because of engine problems, and 3 were shot down by our airborne fighter planes on night patrol. The ack-ack- gunners at Yontan and nearby Kadena shot down 4 more on their approach to the airstrip. Only one commando transport managed to crash land at Yontan as planned -- and only 10 of the 14 suicide commandos emerged in fighting shape.

But, once out of the plane, they ran among the Marine aircraft parked there. They planted the demolition charges and threw grenades. These commandos were all eventually shot and killed – but not before they had destroyed 10 planes, damaged 30, and burned a 70 thousand gallon aviation fuel supply dump.

Kadena was only 3 miles from Yontan, and – not knowing that only one plane had landed -- we were put on alert to expect similar landings and attacks. It was dark, and we got into our Jeeps and bomb trucks and began to slowly drive up and down the airstrip. We were on the lookout both for landings at Kadena – and for possible Japanese infiltrators coming from the landings at Yontan.

We weren't allowed to turn on any lights and make ourselves targets for any Japs moving towards our planes. Suddenly there was a shot. That made everyone start to get off the trucks. The shooter was some guy who shot at one of Okinawa's many goats – thinking it was a Jap.

I jumped off the bomb truck expecting action. Well, on the way down off the truck, I hit my head on some guy's helmet -- and got a black eye for my quick response in getting off the truck and onto the ground. But, once again, our night patrol aircraft and the ack-ack crews had saved us from attack. None of the Kamikaze commandos survived Yontan to reach Kadena.

One day, Lt. Carter landed his Avenger at Kadena after a bombing mission and taxied into his spot on the side of the airstrip. I began the usual post-mission procedure. I checked the tape over the gun muzzles and saw that they were blown away. I next motioned for him to open the bomb bay doors just a crack so that I could check to see if the bomb bay was empty.

But, the bomb bay doors suddenly swung open all the way – and three 265 pound fragmentation bombs fell to the ground with loud thuds. When Lt. Carter and the two gunners heard the bombs hit the ground, they jumped out of the plane. They ran for their lives and caught a getaway ride on a passing Jeep.

Within seconds, the area around the Avenger was deserted – except for me and Willis Knight. The area was suddenly like a ghost town. Seeing no sense in risking both of us, I told Willis to leave the area while I looked at the situation.

I spent a couple of minutes figuring out how this mess happened. In his dive on the target, Lt. Carter had released 6 bombs – but only 3 fell clear of the plane. The bomb release must have malfunctioned and kept the other 3 bombs temporarily hung up in the bomb bay. After Lt. Carter had closed the bomb bay doors and leveled off at the end of the dive, the g forces caused the remaining 3 bombs to fall free of the shackles and land on the bottom of the bomb bay.

So much for how it probably happened. Now the problem was what to do to disarm the bombs. The safety wires had been pulled out as the bombs fell – unlocking their arming propellers. The propellers had to turn 25 revolutions to arm the bomb. The key question was: Did the air wash that blew through the bomb bay during the return flight turn one or more of these propellers almost 25 revolutions?

I guessed that the bombs had fallen onto the closed bomb bay doors, and maybe onto each other, in such a way that the propellers were accidentally jam-locked and couldn't turn -- even in the 100 mph breeze blowing through the closed bomb bay.

This guess was for the best possible outcome. The big unknown was whether or not one of those propellers was within a hair's breadth of having turned 25 revolutions.

I stayed with the bombs and taped all the propellers so that they couldn't move. Then, I slowly unscrewed each fuse and removed each detonator.
(Each fuse had two detonators. The smaller detonator would set off the larger detonator – which would then set off the bomb. You are reading this because my luck held.)

The entire airstrip was now deserted. I took the fuses and detonators back to the ordnance tent where we kept our supplies. There were several guys in the tent, but it was dead quiet in there. I laid the fuses and detonators on the table in front of Tech. Sgt. Mario "Mike" Vecciarelli. He was in charge of the ordnance, and I wanted him to see that the fuses and detonators had been reclaimed, and the 3 bombs were now safe to handle. Then I left.

(Mike was the real thing. He wanted to fight for his country so badly that he forged his birth date so that he just made the maximum age limit for enlistment. As a former Golden Gloves contender from the New York area, he was in good shape and nobody questioned his age. He was an excellent Marine.)

About 15 or 20 minutes later, Mike caught up with me outside. He told me he was going to put me up for a medal, because I had not only risked my life – but I may have saved other lives as well.

To add a little humor to what had been a potentially dangerous situation, he also said I saved the government $28,000 – which was the price of a Grumman Avenger. But I wasn't worried about the plane at the time – I was worried about me.

I told him that I did not think I deserved a medal because I was only doing my job. He waved off my response and said he was going to put me in for a medal anyway.

One day Willis Knight and I went to the bomb dump at Kadena, and we picked up 16 – 500 pound bombs. We put 4 bombs on each of 4 dollies, and connected the dollies in a train to the back of the bomb truck. We began driving across the back of the airstrip. Suddenly, Willis said just one word, "Look!"

I looked up – and saw a Kamikaze flying along the airstrip – heading straight towards us. I knew I didn't even have time to turn off the ignition key on the truck. We both jumped out of the truck – which continued to chug along as we ran for our lives.

The Kamikaze got about one-third of the way down the airstrip when our ack-ack gunners hit it. The plane flipped over and crashed away from the airstrip. We ran back to the truck – which was still chugging along the strip. We climbed on, and pulled over to the side of the airstrip. Then we just sat there for a few minutes – until we could get our wits back together. We were saved again by the ack-ack gunners. Every once in a while, I think of them – and thank them.

The Corsairs and ack-ack gunners had shot down so many Japanese planes that the island was littered with them. They had to push them together with bulldozers into huge piles. There were scrapyards of enemy aircraft everywhere.

One Japanese plane was shot down and crashed near the Kadena airstrip. The force of the impact threw the pilot out of the plane and killed him – breaking many of his bones. His uniform was torn open and we could see that he was wearing a rubber suit underneath it. It was like a cold water pilot's suit, which kept a pilot from suffering hypothermia when they had to ditch in cold seas. Would a Kamikaze pilot need a cold water suit? Perhaps not. The sea around Okinawa was warm in April: We swam in it.

Our best guess was that the Kamikaze pilots wore these suits to slow the rate of bleeding out if they were wounded from gunfire or ack-ack shrapnel during their final approach to the target. Kamikaze pilots would hold their flight path toward certain parts of a target ship to get the maximum effect of the strike. They would fly into a hail of ack-ack and machine gun fire from the target ship. If the pilot was hit, he might gain a few seconds of additional consciousness to keep his plane on target for the last few hundred yards before impact. Pilots going for land targets might do the same.

On July 5th, the Japanese land-based artillery in the south shelled us for a day or so, and one of their shells hit our bomb dump. The rockets in the dump didn't have their warheads on. (We armed them with the warheads and put in the fuses just before we installed them on the planes.) But, the solid fuel rocket motors were in the rocket casings. They were igniting and launching the rockets into the air and spinning them. This went on for 3 days after the initial bombing. It was July 4th back in the states, and I wondered what the folks back home would think if they could see this demonstration of fireworks.

And, every so often one of the bombs in our dump would go off with a big boom. Then another big boom as one bomb would set off another. This went on for 3 days also – until the bomb dump fire finally burned itself out.

One day after we had visited Kin, we began walking south along the road -- hoping to hitch a ride to Kadena. We saw a group of about 5 young women walking north along the road towards us. They could have been refugees or farm workers. They could have been "comfort girls" who had been pressed into serving the Japanese troops as prostitutes. They may have been left behind during the Japanese retreat and were now on their way home. But, something about the situation looked suspicious to me.

When they saw us, these women turned off the road into a field. We could hear them chattering. They were carrying bundles on their heads. They put these bundles on the ground and began taking off their clothes. Then they started waving to us – and beckoning us to come to them.

Were they grateful to us for liberating their island? Or, were they recently-unemployed working girls just trying to make a few bucks to feed themselves? Whatever the case, this looked like some kind of a trap to me. Then an Army truck came along, and we put our thumbs up to hitch a ride. The truck stopped, we got on, and these women shook their fists at us.

Later, we found out that some gangs of women tried to get U.S. troops into positions where Japanese troops could kill them from ambush. I don't know if any of these women volunteered to do this, or were threatened by the Japanese or the conscripted Okinawans. Luckily, we had hitched out and didn't have to find out the hard way if there was an ambush waiting for us.

But, I continued to take chances – going into caves and souvenir hunting. Looking back, I can see that it was crazy. I never came across any Japanese troops on the ground. We were essentially Marine Air support troops located at the airstrips. But, the Japs hunted us from the air -- with Kamikaze planes and long-range land-based artillery. Also, they hunted us at night by infiltrating our tents. Their first target was pilots -- but gunners, ordnance men, and airplane mechanics counted too. We counted because we helped to keep our planes – and our pilots – in the air.

We began to get some 232 replacements at Kadena. One day, one of them ran up to me and said, “There’s a Jap coming down the road, can I shoot him?” I said, “Wait a minute, let me look”. So I went down the road, and here’s this Oki man – he must have been 90 years old – a tiny civilian in a kimono walking with a cane. And the replacement was going to shoot him! I said, “No, no – you don’t shoot civilians”.

And these poor native Okinawans would walk by us and try to be friendly by giving their traditional greeting, ”Ah so, ah so”. And our replacements would respond by saying, “Hey, who are you calling an a--hole?” (They should have taught these replacements a few words of basic Japanese before they got to the Island.)

Marines casually referred to the native Okinawans as “Gooks”. This was their long-time name for East Asians. The term was viewed by some as a racial slur – or at least offensive. But it was not usually meant as one. It was more of a nickname – and easier to say than “Native Okinawans”. This was wartime, and the term “political correctness” wasn’t even known then. Besides, we knew that the Okinawans were victims of a cruel occupation force – and we went out of our way to treat the civilians with compassion. They deserved it.

In fact, the guys had taken to calling me “The Gook” because, every chance I got, I was up in the hills among the natives -- going through caves looking for souvenirs. I would have someone look after my plane, and then I’d travel. I don’t know how many miles away from Kadena or Awase I’d go, but I would hitchhike and walk. I couldn’t get enough of exploring the island – I was just crazy for it. Some guys thought I had “gone Asian”. But, all that I really did was to gather souvenirs and help some civilian ethnic Chinese or Okinawans. They had poor dwellings and very little food. (As a Depression kid, I had been there – and I felt for them.)

I just had to explore. But one time I went into this canyon, and I found an American helmet with a bullet hole right through the middle of the front. That convinced me to get out of that area – and stay out. (It made me wonder if I had unknowingly put myself at risk during my time-off wanderings on the island.)

When there were problems that required translation from the few Japanese prisoners we had, and there were no official translators in the area, they would always call on me. They’d say, “Hey Gook, come over here and interpret this guy.”

I could speak Italian, I took three years of Spanish in high school, and there were a lot of Pennsylvania Germans who came into the barber shops I worked at in York who spoke Pennsylvania Dutch. I had a knack for learning languages ever since I was a kid in New Jersey. I’d almost always manage to get something out of these prisoners that sounded like German – and could usually figure out what they were talking about.

I already said that I brought food to one ethnic Chinese family in Kin. While I hadn't "gone Asian", I did charitable things for certain families. They were caught in the crossfire on a relatively small battlefield. Most were hungry and homeless. During the 82 day battle for their island, 150,000 of them perished through collateral damage caused by the fighting between the Japanese and ourselves.

One day, this sixty–something Okinawan guy walked up to me as I was shaving myself. He introduced himself in pretty good English. He said that as a young man he had emigrated from Okinawa to San Francisco. He had operated his own barber shop there. When he retired, he moved back to Okinawa and bought a house. It was gone now – demolished with so many others. He seemed grateful that we had removed the Japanese. He asked if he could finish shaving me as a token of his thanks. I said that would be fine with me. So, he continued my shave. Just then, one of my buddies whispered something to me that made me wonder about the true politics of the guy who was holding a straight razor against my throat. Who did he think caused him to lose his retirement house and everything else? Did he hold Americans responsible?

I wanted to believe he acted out of appreciation for our help and sacrifices. My heart was with him. But, I chickened out and took back my razor -- and I thanked him for the offer. With so much uncertainty as to how he really felt – I could trust him only so far.

Warrant Officer Estes Ratliffe was also on Okinawa with 232. And, he still had Lady, the dog who was the mother of Judy. She had another litter, and I got one of the pups. I named her Judy 2. The Okinawans acted as though she would make a great item for dinner. (Dogs were eaten all over the Pacific.) I thought, "Don't look at my dog that way – she is not on the menu."

One day the escort carrier Gilbert Islands anchored offshore. This is the carrier that my good buddy Bob Messmer was assigned to when we completed ordnance training at Santa Barbara. We were both in Ordnance Squadron 143 at Santa Barbara, but when they split the squadron in two, Bob remained in 143 and was assigned to the Gilbert Islands. I was transferred from 143 to land-based Squadron 232 – together with the one half of Squadron 143. Some of the 143 guys on the carrier wanted to see old friends from the Santa Barbara days who were onshore with guys from 143 and 232.

Bob Messmer wasn't with the first party that came to the beach to visit for just a few hours. (He had applied for a pass, but wasn't listed for the first group to go ashore.) There were about 8 ordnance guys who were accompanied by a Corsair pilot who wanted to step on Okinawan soil. He was an "Indian boy". I don't remember his name, but – as was the good-natured custom at the time – everyone called Native American pilots "Chief". He was a very down-to-earth guy and mixed well with the enlisted men.

I had gone to the beach with a Japanese book I had found on one of my travels and wanted to give to Bob Messmer. As he wasn't there, I asked the Corsair pilot if he would take it to the Gilbert Islands and give it to Bob Messmer as a souvenir of Okinawa. He thanked me and said that he would do so.

After this group had gone back to the Gilbert Islands, I exercised my spirit of adventure – and my luck -- and went to see Major Feldmeier. I asked him for permission to visit Bob Messmer on the carrier. Without hesitation, he said that I could. I asked him how long I could stay, and he said, "As long as you want." I had just invited myself onto the carrier – and felt pretty good about it. And, they had given me written orders that OK'd the visit.

Somebody explained to me how to get to the carrier on one of the small shuttle boats. They told me that when I got to the carrier, the first thing to do as you step out of the boat onto the steps is to salute the flag. Then, after climbing the stairs, you salute the officer there as you step onto the deck. Nobody on the ship questioned me. And, here came my old buddy, Bob Messmer.

He took me on a tour of the ship – showing me the plane elevators and how the carrier operated. I saw the Corsairs below decks with their wings folded. He took me to chow and got me a bunk for overnight. We tried to catch up with each other as to what we had been doing since Santa Barbara. But, on a busy ship like a carrier – and with so much to see -- you don't have enough time to talk about everywhere you've been and everything you've done since the split-up of the squadrons.

I spent the night on the carrier, but the next morning I got the old "duty calls" itch. I told Bob that I had to get back to the base. He asked me to stay longer. But, despite Major Feldmeier's offer to stay "as long as you want", I couldn't shake the feeling that there were Avengers to be serviced. (I was in a group of 4 ordnance guys, and we worked to arm 4 Avengers in rotation.)

I had gotten to visit the carrier and see Bob Messmer. My main missions had been accomplished, and I just had the urge to get back to the airstrip. I took the small boat back to shore.

Messmer wrote me a letter a few weeks later. He said it was a good thing I returned to shore when I did, because there was a sudden typhoon warning right after I left. They weighed anchor and headed to the China Sea to protect the carrier from being beached or otherwise damaged. Some guys who had stayed a couple of days were still on board when they sailed. They headed to China, and they were still at sea about a month later.

After the Japanese had been driven to a small last-stand area at the very southern tip of the island, we would go south to look around. One time we went to the Shuri Castle. It was originally the seat of the Okinawan kings, and later home of the Okinawan government. The place had been leveled by the huge guns of the battleship U.S.S. Mississippi. She had anchored off the south coast of the island, and the Shuri Castle was within range. Only two buildings were left standing. One was the Treasury building, and the other was a small church with a cross on top.

All around the ruins of Shuri Castle, there were pieces of stuffed animals. There must have been a museum of natural history in the castle, and it had native animals stuffed by taxidermy for the exhibits.

We also went to see the capital city of Naha -- a short distance west of the Shuri Castle. It, too, had been leveled. It had been the site of the Japanese artillery school. They had trained all the Japanese artillery officers there. They had the target coordinates of every square foot of Okinawa laid out. That was probably the reason that their artillery shots against us were so accurate.

On the road north from Shuri and Naha, we saw many dead Japanese soldiers along the road. Marine and Army details had laid all these dead Japanese soldiers in orderly rows and buried them with care. They didn't just dig a trench and bulldoze them into it. They showed all this respect, and – to tell the truth – it surprised me. Why would we spend all this time and care to bury Japs? But, strangely, it was even a little sad to see all these enemy dead.

I remembered seeing this one Japanese lying there. He was well-built, and I realized that his mother was never going to see him again. Even though they were a hated enemy, there's a certain amount of sorrow for an individual soldier who has died for his country. I have always thought that we were all children of God. It was a shame that people had to die in war.

But, this was a just war. The invasions of so many countries and the attacks on civilians in both the European and Pacific theaters could not be tolerated. And, above all, there was Pearl Harbor.

There was an American flag on a hill near the Awase airstrip. Once, when the work load had slowed, I had a one week assignment to lower the flag at sunset. One night when I was there, a Jeep pulled up with 4 or 5 guys in it. A guy jumped out of the Jeep and yelled, "Hey Frank!"

I looked at this guy and didn't recognize him. I saw from his uniform that he was in the Navy Shore Patrol. I looked closer, and saw that he was Buddy Butera from York. We had graduated from high school together. This was the first time I had seen him on Okinawa. He had grown a beard, and he had an earring in his ear. He had what looked like blood on his face below the earring, so I asked him what happened to him.

He said they got him drunk one night, and they took a Mercury dime and cut out the Mercury head and the rim around the coin. Then they pierced his ear and put on the earring. Then they put Methylate on his face to guard against infection – and to make him look as though he had been wounded.

I told Buddy about my "hobby" – getting Jap rifles and bayonets as souvenirs -- and trading them to the Navy guys for food. He thought this was a good operation. He partnered with me, and we'd gather the souvenirs and take them down to the beach where the ships would come in. And they gave us all kinds of real food – including canned food and hamburger -- in exchange for the Jap souvenirs.

Buddy lived up on the hill behind our tents. We were getting so much food in trades for Japanese souvenirs that we couldn't eat it all. And we began to share it with his fellow Shore Patrol guys. We'd load up one of our trucks, and we'd take food to Buddy's group.

We'd work together now and then – and we had plenty of good food for the duration. I sometimes wonder what stories were told back in the States when the Navy guys showed these souvenirs to their family and friends. I brought home one of the bayonets, but I didn't bring home any of the Japanese rifles. I wasn't a hunter, and I didn't trust their workmanship. They had roughly turned surfaces. By contrast, our rifles were very smooth. Some guys took Japanese rifles home to use for deer hunting. But I wouldn't shoot one of the Japanese rifles: I was afraid it might blow up in my face.

The war on Okinawa was winding down. The Japanese forces in the last small area were being systematically annihilated by U.S. forces. The top Japanese officers had committed hara-kiri. (Ritual suicide.) I loaded leaflets into the bomb bays of our Avengers showing instructions on how to surrender. These were dropped to the remaining Japanese troops. The leaflets assured their safety, but most ignored the offer. Many enlisted Japanese soldiers committed suicide by holding a grenade to their stomach. They would rather die for the Emperor than live to rebuild a ruined Japan. We Marines never understood that.

Squadron VMTB-232 flew their last strike mission on Okinawa on 19 July 1945. Okinawa was "officially secured" on 21 July. We guessed that plans for invading the main islands of Japan had been made, and that it was only a matter of time before a new invasion fleet would be assembled.

Back at Awase, we continued to service our Avengers. But, the pilots flew only a few ground support supply missions. Most of the ground fighting was over. But the Corsairs at Awase were still flying patrols. And, they flew along as fighter cover on some of the bomber strike missions against the main islands of Japan -- and nearby smaller islands having military targets.

During this time, we lost one Avenger – the pilot and both gunners. I don't think they were shot down: I think they had engine failure and went into the sea. They searched for them – but couldn't find them.

Okinawa was now available as a base for long-range heavy bombers that could reach Japan. (Getting a base for long-range bombers was one of the key reasons for invading Okinawa.)

We were curious as to what long-range bombers were now being based and serviced at Kadena. So, we jumped into a bomb truck and drove over there. We saw that they had B-25 Mitchell medium bombers, together with B17 Flying Fortress and B-24 Liberator heavy bombers. But they didn't have any B-29 Superforts: They were based on the islands of Saipan and Tinian.

One of the Army Air Force pilots now at Kadena invited us to come in and look around. He even invited us to climb into some of the planes. But, we told him we really didn't want to do that. For some reason, we didn't feel that the Army Air Force was our territory, and we felt odd about getting into their planes. I don't know why we felt that way, but we did.

The air war had now bypassed Okinawa. The Japanese fighters were busy protecting mainland targets -- seaports, airports, and weapons plants – from our bombers. Very rarely did they fly to Okinawa.

The air war soon settled into bombing runs on Japan by the B–29's. They were dropping incendiary bombs on many cities on the Japanese mainland. One night they ignited a firestorm that burned Tokyo, causing 100,000 casualties. Still, there was no indication that the Japanese were going to surrender.

Then, on 06 August, an Air Force B-29 named "Enola Gay" flew from the island of Tinian and dropped an atomic bomb on Hiroshima – a city near the southern tip of Honshu, the largest island of Japan. We didn't know what an A-bomb was, but the claim was that it was the most powerful bomb ever invented. They thought this fearsome weapon would force Japan to surrender. We listened to the radio, but the only thing the Japanese said was that *they* also had an A-bomb -- and they were going to drop it on the U.S. troops on Okinawa.

By this time, we had heard some details of the awesome destructive power of the A-bomb. And, we didn't know whether to believe the Japs or not. Marine

Command alerted us and said to be prepared for anything -- because the Japanese were probably going to attack us with whatever they had.

There must not have been a response from the Japanese government to our demand that they surrender unconditionally. Then, on 09 August, the Air force dropped a second A-bomb on the city of Nagasaki – on the southernmost island of Kyushu. A week went by, and there was still no news of further hostilities – or peace plans.

Late on the night of 16 August, I was at the outdoor movie theater when I heard gunfire begin. And I thought, here come the Japs. I picked up Judy 2 and headed for our tents. I ran across the rice paddies – falling in along the way.

I heard scattered small arms fire followed by salvos from our ships offshore. Their 16 inch guns were booming out across the water. My first thought was that the Japanese had mounted a big attack in retaliation for our A-bombs.

As I reached our tents, I ran into this guy who was firing a Thomson submachine gun. I asked him what was going on, and he said, "The war is over, the war is over!"

Then I realized that there wasn't any sound of 16 inch shells screaming overhead. They hadn't armed the guns on our ships with shells, just with gunpowder bags. These were victory shots – but the noise was deafening.

When I got back to my tent, Judy 2 was yelping in pain because the noise was hurting her ears. I laid on the ground and covered her ears to protect them from the noise. There were tracer bullets flying everywhere. The day before, they had strung electric wires around the tent compound to give us lights. The bullets were so thick, they cut the wires – and everything went dark. The next morning I examined our tent: It was full of bullet holes.

I heard that 18 guys got killed by the stray bullets of our own V-J Day celebration fire that night.

The next morning, some of the fighter pilots were celebrating with mock dogfights. I saw 2 Mustang fighters engaged in a mock duel – and they collided. Both planes went down into the sea. I saw one pilot's chute open. His was the only one. The other pilot didn't get out and was probably killed on impact.

I also heard that about 16 guys got killed celebrating that following day. What do you tell the parents when their son is killed after the war is over? Do you say he had been killed in action? And how do you explain that they were killed by friendly fire in celebration of the War's end?

There was still some sniping and shelling from Japanese holdouts on Okinawa. And, our artillery exploded a Japanese bomb dump somewhere south of the Shuri line.

The war was basically over -- in the air, on the sea, and on the ground. We no longer had much of anything to do. Our Avengers remained on the ground at Awase. The war had passed us by as it had moved north. We hung around our tents – and we continued to scrounge for food.

Judy 2 caught distemper, and it crippled her. She eventually began to drag her hind legs – and could no longer function. With much regret, we had to put her down with a shot of morphine – and she went to sleep. It was sad to think that I had lost both Judys.

I dug a hole, buried Judy 2, and put decorative stones on her grave. The Okinawans would come and look at the grave with some curiosity. Perhaps they thought this burial for a dog had religious meaning for Americans.

They had looked at Judy 2 longingly when she was alive. The Okis had eaten dogs in peacetime. The food shortages in wartime must have made her all the more tempting. I guess they thought it was a waste to bury a tasty pup. We gave them K rations, but they may have longed for traditional food on occasion.

There were times when we had lulls. I'd get some of my buddies to look after my plane, and I'd tour the island. The souvenirs I'd collect were now food coupons for us.

The Japanese signed the unconditional surrender document on the deck of the battleship U.S.S. Missouri on 02 September, 1945. The Japanese plan to cause so many American casualties on Okinawa that they could sue for peace -- and avoid unconditional surrender -- had failed.

And, best of all, there was no longer a need to invade Japan! The official estimate of lives saved in the U.S. armed forces was 500,000 to 1,000,000. And the casualties among the Japanese military and civilian populations would have been enormous.

I and my buddies of 232 were glad that we would not be part of these numbers. We were glad that we had survived and were looking forward to going home. But we had one last big adventure. In early October, Typhoon Louise came to Okinawa with high winds and 60 - 70 foot waves. We could sit on the ground with our backs to the wind – and we couldn't fall over backwards. Later, Willis Knight and I were walking down a hill in the torrential rain from the Typhoon. The ground was a clay soil – and very slippery. He lost his footing and went rolling down the hill. I was reminded of Leno Sacco and his tumble a couple of months earlier -- when a Japanese plane chased us from the movie.

I began to laugh – just as I had done when Leno went down. And Willis said he didn't think it was funny. I made it worse by saying it looked funny. And now Willis is really upset with me. (I just hadn't learned my lesson.)

But, just then, the Quonset huts near us began to rumble and move along the ground from the increasing strength of the wind. Worse yet, pieces of the galvanized steel skin began to be torn loose from the Quonset huts and be whirled through the air by the wind. At that moment, we forgot about everything else except getting into some shelter to protect us from being cut in half by these flying pieces of sheet steel.

We saw one Quonset hut begin to slide over the edge of a cliff. We looked for cover, and we found something that looked as though it had been a type of bomb shelter. It was a small concrete bunker, and it seemed to be secured to the ground. We went in there – and that's where we stayed for a couple of days until Louise moved out to sea.

Okinawa was leveled by the typhoon. The tents were down – as were many of the huts and flimsy buildings. Many ships had been at anchor in Buckner Bay on the Pacific side. The storm had changed course, and the warning came to Okinawa too late to allow the ships to be moved out to sea in time. They were trapped and at the mercy of the wind and waves. Some were beached, some were smashed into each other, some were dashed on the reef and battered, and some were sunk. The ships' crews had fought the typhoon's waves by running the engines and trying to power the ships into the waves – but the sea surges overwhelmed them. It was good that this disaster didn't happen a few months earlier when the battle for Okinawa was just beginning. The casualty list of U.S. ships was long – with more ships damaged by this typhoon than by any battle in the Pacific during WW II.

Many damaged ships had to be sunk because they were not worth repairing. The ships that had been swept onto the beach had to be pulled off with winches and cables from ships that still floated. Many had been damaged by the action of the tremendous waves.

Many of our planes were damaged – and some destroyed. The wind had lifted them in their tie-down cables and repeatedly slammed them into the air strip. By some miracle – or coincidence -- there were replacement supplies of tents, food, and medicine on the way to Okinawa before Louise hit. We had a new tent compound in a relatively short time.

After this typhoon, we didn't have much to do but clean up. Afterwards, we hung around our tents, and continued to hunt souvenirs. We took them to the beach and traded them to the remaining Navy guys for food. The Sailors were still eager to get Japanese rifles and bayonets.

The war was now focused on the occupation of Japan. I began to think back on what a good unit we had become -- and what we had accomplished. It seemed to me that we had done a good job.

And yet, we were all – I don't know -- a little crazy. I guess this was partly because of the stress of sudden dangers from the artillery fire, the Kamikazes, and the night infiltrators who we thought would steal into our tents and cut our throats. These were the worst threats, and we never knew when they would happen -- or from which direction they would come.

But, we managed to treat everything as a joke: We got shot at, we got bombed, we got shelled – and we came out of our fox holes laughing. Just crazy.

Suddenly, they announced that those in VMTB - 232 with 55 service points were going home!

And that included me.

Chapter 11

Going Home

At Awase, we gathered in a supply tent to get the uniforms we were to wear on the voyage home. They had large benches on which they had put piles of clothing – including long underwear. We thought they were crazy. We had always been at sea in the tropics! Who needed long underwear? So, we didn't take them. We didn't understand that the ocean voyage home would circle north along the Aleutian Islands – near Alaska. And it got so cold there we almost froze!

We were transported in landing craft from the beach at Awase to the troopship Okanogan, anchored offshore. We sailed from Okinawa on 15 November 1945. At last, we were on the way home.

(Willis Knight didn't go with us. You needed 55 service points to go home, and he had only 50. They sent him to Japan to continue his service. But, he caught up with us in San Diego about 3 weeks after we got there.)

We were at sea about 15 days. I didn't stand at the rail and watch the marine life like I did when we sailed to Guadalcanal. And the guys weren't very active. Some would play cards, but most would just hang around. I think most of them were thinking about the hardships and danger of the past year, the guys that didn't make it, and our good fortune in having survived. And, they began to wonder about the uncertainties of the civilian life ahead.

There was one near-casualty on the voyage. A sailor jumped overboard somewhere along the west coast of Canada. He was yelling that he was not going home. He was saying something about trouble with his wife. So, they searched the ocean for him. It was night, and they used searchlights. They found his white sailor cap floating on the surface. After 2 hours, they found him – and he was still alive! (Had the war still been on, they probably wouldn't have stopped for him.)

We were supposed to land at San Francisco, but there was a dock strike there.

Why? We were just on the way home from winning a war! In my opinion, their timing was bad. They probably had a band and a celebration waiting for us at San Francisco. We were diverted to San Pedro -- the seaport just south of Los Angeles.

It was foggy as we were coming into the docks at San Pedro. We were standing at the bow rail – waiting to catch site of our home shore. Suddenly, we heard the captain cussing up a storm. He threw the Okanogan into reverse. The ship shuddered from the reversing of the screws, and we started to slow down. Sensing an impending collision, we ran back, away from the bow. The other ship missed us by just a few feet. It never slowed nor took any evasive action. The captain of the Okanogan continued cussing out the captain of the other ship – calling him every name in the book.

We were lucky – because it would have been a stupid way for us to end the war. We had made it through the biggest, longest, highest-casualty battle of WW II. To think that we might have gotten killed in a collision with a friendly ship on the approach to the dock as we were coming into a home port was strange. That would not have been a good ending. But, it was better to have bad luck in California than to have had it on Okinawa.

After the excitement, we landed at San Pedro. The Salvation Army was there to greet us with doughnuts and a container of milk. We then got on troop trucks for the drive to the Marine base at San Diego – which was about 200 miles south of San Pedro.

So, we rode south in this long truck convoy. After a while the guys asked the driver to pull over so they could have a pit stop. The truck driver said, "The convoy doesn't stop – for any reason." The guys said, "If you don't stop, we're going to piss out the back of the truck!" The truck driver replied, "I don't care what you do, the convoy doesn't stop."

Well, the guys lined up at the back of the truck and began relieving themselves onto the highway. Almost immediately, the guys were doing this from every truck – and the pavement was getting wet. Luckily, I had kept my milk container. I used it as a urinal, then emptied it out the side of the truck.

This behavior did not go unnoticed. I remember 3 young girls in a convertible who were driving by the convoy in the passing lane. They were laughing hysterically at the show. You can imagine the scene: The pavement was getting wetter as the guys in all the trucks joined the rolling pit stop. The convoy drivers began to turn on their windshield wipers as the trucks rolled along the ever-wetter pavement. And the girl driving the convertible turned on her wipers, too. (When you next hear the expression, "Whizzing down the highway", think of the guys of 232.)

When we got to San Diego, we first went to a tent where they gave each of us a whole new uniform. The clothes we got when we left Awase were now a little the worse for wear from the sea voyage. They were badly wrinkled from all that lying around and wondering what things were going to be like at home.

What was odd about getting the new uniforms was the way they were handed out. There were women Marines there, and they sized you up as you were approaching the tables piled with clothing. They didn't ask you your size, they just threw clothes at you. And, they fit. It was unbelievable: they knew just what size you wore by looking at you. Then, they quickly measured your feet – and the shoes fit also.

The method of dispensing the uniforms reminded us of the way our first dungarees and shoes were handed out at boot camp. They took no measurements there either. They just eyeballed you and threw the clothes and shoes at you – and they fit. We got the same treatment coming home as we did when we joined the Marines.

Then we went into the next tent, and they told us about the arrangements for transportation home. There were some other instructions, but I don't remember them all.

Next, we went to the base and they gave us medications for whatever ailed us. Then we were in a building with 2 levels of bunks – one over the other. Suddenly, we heard the "whooshing" sound of a big artillery shell coming in. The guys who were trying out their bunks dove out, and we all got flat on the floor.

But, there was no explosion. So, everybody said, "What the hell was that?" One of the guys from the base who was giving us instructions about going home said, "That's a jet airplane." We had never seen or even heard of a jet airplane before. So, the guy from the base told us the basics about jets. They were new, and they were powered by a new type of engine – a turbojet.

Some of the first jet planes were being test flown from the Navy airfields around San Diego. They weren't operational yet, they were still undergoing development trials. And we didn't understand how they could fly without that old reliable Hamilton propeller on the front to pull them along.

Then, to keep us busy, they'd have work details for us. Every morning, we'd have to fall in to be assigned to do work around the base. If we didn't feel good, they'd give us aspirin – or something like that.

We'd all line up and act like we didn't feel good. They'd give us our pills and watch to see that we took them. Then, they'd give us the rest of the day off. After months of lifting bombs, I opted for the days off.

We were there only a week or two, and then they gave us a 30 day furlough to go home. We were to travel by train. When we went to get on the train to Chicago, the conductor said there were no more seats available. So, we said we were on furlough, what are we to do? The conductor said, “Well, do you want to ride in the club car?” We said, “Yeah, we’ll ride in the club car.” There were nice soft seats in there. And, there was a bar. So, a group of maybe 8 of us went into the club car. And that’s where we slept – on those nice soft seats. (They were much nicer than the hard seats I tried to sleep on during the train ride from York to Parris Island.)

And whenever we were approaching the state line of a dry state, the conductor would say, “If anyone wants a drink or a beer, get it now – because as soon as we cross the line, the bar closes”. I didn’t drink beer, but some guys did, and they’d have to watch their locations to keep from going without – especially when we were approaching big states that took hours to cross.

When we got to Chicago, I tried to call home to tell them when I was coming. But, there was always a line at the pay phones in the train stations – and the trains didn’t wait. We didn’t have a phone at home, and I would have had to call a neighbor. But the neighbor’s phones were almost all 4 party lines then, and they were always busy.

The odds of getting through under these conditions were slim to none. So, I caught the train from Chicago to Harrisburg and trusted my luck. Getting home shouldn’t be a problem for someone who had recently explored much of Okinawa.

I got off the train at Harrisburg and began to hitch a ride to York. I was picked up by a truck driver, and he took me as far as North York. He let me off at the Codorus Bridge on North George Street. From there, I began to walk toward my house in the “Little Italy” section of downtown York.

There was a pool hall on the way home where a lot of my buddies used to hang out. I stopped in just to see who was there, and to say hello and let them know I was home on furlough. There was one buddy who was sort of a wise guy. As I was being welcomed back by the other guys with handshakes and backslaps, he lit a firecracker and threw it on the floor behind me. When the firecracker went off, I hit the floor. This was a test to see if I had actually been in combat. I was really upset that they pulled that trick on me. I got up and stormed out – and they knew I was mad.

Then I walked the few blocks more – and I was home on Cherry Alley. There was much hugging – and a few tears from the family -- when I appeared in the doorway. They had no idea when I was coming home, so it was a surprise. By chance, some of my neighborhood friends were there also. I was home at last.

While I was in the Pacific, my mother had made a promise to God in her prayers. She promised to have a big "Welcome Home" celebration dinner for me. It was important to my parents that the only son of poor Sicilian immigrants had returned alive and well from the hell that was Okinawa.

So, about a week before Christmas, my mother invited family, friends and neighbors to our house for the dinner. We had about 25 people – and they filled the house. About 4 or 5 women came early to help her cook. I can't remember how many dishes they cooked – but there were many.

Every table we had was lined up to make a long, communal setting. Some people had to eat sitting on chairs in the kitchen and living room. I was seated at the head of the table in my Marine uniform. And there was no time lost by family, friends or neighbors finding seats so that certain ones could sit together. Everyone sat as one community – because they all knew each other.

The scene looked like a Norman Rockwell painting of a soldier's homecoming – Sicilian style. There were no testimonials or speeches. And, I don't remember being asked to say anything. With this wonderful feast on the table, we just said grace and dug in.

After dinner, this celebration for my safe return continued as everyone sat and talked. There were stories of how the family, the friends -- and the neighborhood -- endured the war. I thought to myself how fortunate I was to come back to such a warm and happy home. I hoped that all of my buddies in the Marine Corps had this kind of happy homecoming.

I spent the next few days visiting family and friends. My sister Josephine was in the York Hospital expecting her first child. She had the baby, a girl, during my furlough. They named the baby Frances. Her husband was in the Marine Corps, but he was in Hawaii and couldn't get home for the birth. After I had visited Josephine in the hospital, I stopped on the walk home to see some friends and neighbors to tell them about the new baby.

At one barber shop in the neighborhood, I planned a short stop to tell the barber and his wife about Frances. Their name was Randisi and they spoke Italian in their home. They were delighted that I could carry on our conversation entirely in Italian. I was ready to leave, but the barber kept asking me to stay until their daughter got home from work. Time went by, and this began to look like a plot to introduce me to a daughter of marriageable age. This made me feel a little odd. So I said, "No, no, I've really got to go." And I left.

When my furlough was over, I took the train to Cherry Point, North Carolina – to the Marine Aviation Separation Unit. There, on January 30, 1946, I was honorably discharged from the United States Marine Corps – with the rank of

corporal. I was credited with having participated in the Okinawa Campaign, the Philippines Islands Campaign, and in the Air Operation Against Japan.
And, I received $100 in mustering out pay – plus 5 cents per mile to return from Cherry Point to York. My monthly rate of pay when discharged was $66.

(Best of all, I did not owe the government $28,000 for one Grumman Avenger!)

I was now a civilian again. I would need to gather the necessities of the civilian life: more education, a job, a wife and a family.

CHAPTER 12

The Return to Civilian Life

The end of WW II brought layoffs at companies all over the country. York was no exception. With the war work done, vets who had jobs before the war tried to get them back. Vets who didn't have jobs before the war found that there were almost no jobs available. I thought that something would become available within a year.

The government set up the "52-20 club" – which provided vets with $20 a week for 52 weeks. It was a form of temporary unemployment insurance for returning veterans. Each week, we went to a bank in York and showed our discharge papers. They gave us our $20, but first they always asked us, "Haven't you found a job *yet*?" It was apparently going to take time to sort out the switch from wartime to peacetime production demands, and the job-seeking vets were supposed to get by on $20 a week.

For my personal job insurance in this uncertain time, I planned to go to Harrisburg to take my barber test. But first, I went back to work part-time for Tony Rizzuto to work the few remaining months required to complete my apprenticeship. He now had a barber shop in the 200 block of West Market Street.

After completing these hours, I went to Harrisburg to take my barber licensing test. I didn't have a car, so I asked my friend Pete Terroso to drive me to Harrisburg. The test was given in an examining barber's shop. I had taken Buddy Butera along as my "customer". While the barber watched, I gave Buddy the "works": a haircut, shave, shampoo, and massage – every service that was usually offered in a barber shop.

I passed the exam, and the barber who gave me the test asked me to come to work for him. But, I didn't have a car, and I didn't want to commute from York to Harrisburg. When we arrived back in York, a cop gave Pete a ticket for turning left on the yellow. I think he must have seen us as crazy young guys wasting time and in need of a lesson. We couldn't tell him that we were just happy about my passing the barber test on my first try. Anyway, I gave Pete the money to pay his ticket.

Then, I continued part time work in Tony's shop. He didn't pay me very much, but at least he paid me. After a year or so, he added another barber. But, the number of customers didn't increase fast enough to keep all 3 of us busy and making decent money.

My earnings went down, so I left Tony and went to work in a shop across the street for a barber named John Lucia. Tony was upset with me, but I hadn't told any of my customers that I was leaving – or where I was going. So, Tony couldn't complain that I was taking customers with me.

In the meantime, I continued my education by taking more machine shop courses through the financial support of the G.I. Bill. I went back to the Atreus Wanner Vocational School to get more training in machine shop subjects. In June 1946 I received a certificate for blue print reading – and another for Machine Shop Practice. In November 1947, I received a certificate for the completion of 2,433 hours of Machine Tool Operation.

Now that I had this additional training in machine shop practices, I began to look for industrial work. I was offered a job with one of the largest companies in York. But, they wanted to assign me to a field branch in Chicago – and I didn't want to leave York.

Then I found a half-time job in York with the York Hoover Body Co. One of their divisions made custom bodies for trucks and buses. My first assignment was with the truck body division. My job was to do the final inspection of their telephone truck bodies.

These bodies were custom-fitted with shelves, drawers, and storage compartments for the telephone equipment carried in the trucks. The customers for these trucks included the various regional branches of AT&T. They also made bodies for the York Telephone Company -- a small telephone company that served York County.

With the training I had received in my machine shop courses, and the experience I had gained in the Marine Air Corps Ordnance Group, I had developed a knack for knowing when something was right or wrong in the assembly of equipment. And, I usually had ideas as to what it would take to correct the problems.

When I began this job, I saw that there were always at least 10 – 15 telephone trucks parked outside the plant in a special area. This was the repair lot – and these were the trucks that had failed final in-house inspection and had to be reworked. It seemed to me that there were too many trucks in this lot. As I began to inspect the trucks coming from the assembly area, I saw that there were several key errors in the assembly process.

One typical problem was the welds that were supposed to hold equipment shelves to the inner walls of the body. Many of these welds were not properly made – and not strong enough to bear the weight of the parts and equipment the shelves had to carry. Too many trucks had to be sent back to the weld line to repair this defect. And, the re-welding of the shelves burned the paint. The truck then had to be sent back to the paint line to have the burned areas repainted.

I began to reject every truck with bad welds – and other assembly errors. The telephone companies would inspect the trucks before they would accept them – and reject the ones that were not to their specs. I felt it was just good business to identify and repair the problem trucks before the telephone company inspectors saw them.

Some guys in the production department didn't like this arrangement because I didn't allow any truck to pass unless it was right. I was making $.85 an hour, but the assemblers who were causing the problems were making $1.15 an hour. (And, they were also making $1.15 an hour to correct their own mistakes.)

I asked to be transferred to the assembly shop – because I could use the additional income. My supervisor told me that I was doing such a good job inspecting the trucks that the repair lot was now empty. He said that they couldn't afford to take me off inspection. I then said that this was reason enough that I should make as much as the assemblers. I felt that I was paying my way by saving the cost of reworks.

But, they insisted that I stay with the inspection – and at the same pay rate. They also told me that I could have the next assembly job that became available. Well, several new hires were put on the assembly line as jobs opened up there. Being bypassed like this looked fishy to me, and I never got an acceptable explanation as to what the reasoning behind this decision was.

So, as much as I liked working with mechanical equipment, I didn't like the way things were going. There were some shop politics here that I just didn't understand. And, the inspection job remained half-time only – with no sign of increased hours. And, the pay remained the same -- at $.85 an hour.

As a result, I decided not to fight this problem. I thought I could make more money at barbering – so I quit York Hoover. I thought the chances of being recognized and rewarded for the quality and quantity of my work would be better as a barber.

I then got a job as the resident barber at the Lafayette Club in the first block of East Market Street – just a block from the York city square. This was a prestigious assignment: York was where the Marquis de Lafayette, while visiting York in 1778, proposed a toast to defuse the attempt by the Conway Cabal to unseat George Washington as the General of the Continental Army.

This gave the Lafayette Club name both a historical identity and widespread name recognition. And, it was only a few steps from the Chamber of Commerce and the Yorktowne Hotel. The club was a convenient place for members and guests to meet and talk about the issues of the day. Much of the business and politics of York was discussed there.

But, there turned out to be one major drawback to the job at the Club. The shop also had a manicurist. She would manicure the customers' nails while they were sitting in the barber chair and I cut their hair. I could do a head in 20 minutes – but it took her 45 minutes to do the manicure. I could have cut a second customer in the time it took her to finish the first customer.

The loss in revenue became a problem. Maybe two separate chairs would have helped, but that was not the way it was done there. I came up with what I thought was a solution.

The shop was located in the basement and had both an internal entrance from the club and a walk-down entrance from North Duke Street. When I had gaps in the schedule, I would accept walk-in customers from the street. The Club didn't like that: They wanted the shop to be available on demand for members and their guests. They had a point, but it meant that I couldn't cut hair when I wasn't busy with a Club member or guest.

One day, a new customer named Frank Russo walked in from the street for a haircut. I didn't know him – or that he was a barber with a shop several blocks away on West Market Street. And, I didn't know that this was in fact my "tryout". He was looking for another barber to work in his shop.

When the haircut was done, he thanked me -- and immediately offered me a job! I was surprised, but I accepted. He was the only barber at his shop at the time, and I wasn't put off by the fact that I would have to help develop repeat customers. I had a good feeling about him – because he struck me from the first as being sincere and honest.

So, I said goodbye to the Lafayette Club and went to work for Frank Russo. The working conditions were good at his shop, and we were always busy. He was a very fair employer – and a fine gentleman. I hoped to work there for many years.

Frank Russo had an interesting mix of customers. There were many shop folks and engineers from the York Corporation's offices on Roosevelt Avenue, M.D.'s from "Doctors Row" along West Market Street, lawyers, merchants – a cross section of men mostly from the West York area. And I enjoyed talking with the customers. I learned a great many things from them.

Frank Russo was the brother-in-law of John Grimek – who was a competitive weightlifter. John worked for the internationally-known weightlifting coach and promoter Bob Hoffman. Bob had a company in York that made barbells and packaged nutritional foods. John had been Mr. America a couple of times in the years just before the War. Frank Russo always cut his hair.

Bob Hoffman brought many promising weightlifters to York to be trained in his gym for competition in national and international events. Bob promoted York as the "Weightlifting Capital of the World". And, he was the coach of the U.S. Olympic weightlifting team.

In 1950, a young guy named Steve Reeves arrived in York to train with Bob Hoffman for bodybuilding competition. I cut his hair for several years – during which time he won the Mr. America title once, and the Mr. Universe title twice. Then Steve left York to seek his fortune. And Bob Hoffman made *his* fortune selling barbells to young guys who wanted to look like John Grimek and Steve Reeves.

(Years later, my son Joe asked me to take him to see the action hero movie, "Hercules". As I was watching this movie, I suddenly recognized Hercules: He was Steve Reeves! I was always amazed by the width of his neck. It had taken me forever to cut the hair across the back of it. I told my son that I had cut his hair during the years he had trained in York. This was probably my one meeting with a movie star-to-be. I found out later that Steve Reeves had made 20-plus action hero-type movies -- all featuring his Mr. Universe body.)

Things were beginning to look up for me. I was making good money at Frank Russo's shop. I now had a steady, well-paying job. But, there was still the matter of a wife and family.

One Sunday at church shortly afterward, I saw Mrs. Randisi walk in – followed by her daughter Concetta. Also known as Ginger, Concetta was wearing a black suit, a fuscia turban, and high heels. She was a knockout!

Suddenly, I had a flashback to when I had first seen mother and daughter together. It was before the War. I was working in the vegetable section of the Giant food market on South George Street. Concetta was following her mother then, too. I remember that she was wearing a home-made wool dress, and her hair was cut in the shingle-style popular at the time. I was 15 at the time – and Concetta was 12.

She was still a kid, somewhat self-conscious, and under the age of interest to this "much-older" kid of 15.

But, since I had seen her in the Giant those five years before, she had grown into a lovely young woman. And, the strangest twist of fate? *She* was the daughter that I didn't wait to meet in Randisi's barber shop while I was home on my Christmas furlough in 1945!

Now, I realized that many guys would be after her, and I had better get to meet her as soon as I could.

So, we had our introductions and courted. We were married in June of 1947. We had two fine children: MaryJo was born in 1949, and Joseph in 1954. They both graduated from York College and became accomplished adults. They went on to have fine families of their own. Their children are achievers. I am very proud of my grandchildren. In short, my family life is wonderful.

(An interesting perspective to my life appeared in 1998. That's when Tom Brokaw of NBC News wrote a book about guys like me who grew up with the hard times of the Great Depression and then fought in WW II. The title of his book is, "The Greatest Generation". I came to understand that I was in fact a member of this generation, and I wanted to tell the personal story of my experiences during that period in our nation's history. Mine is just one story of the millions that contributed to that history. My story may not be of major importance, but it would be unique -- and I wanted to make sure that it was finally told in writing – and available to my descendants.)

CHAPTER 13

My Own Shop

In 1954, Concetta's father, Vincenzo, was still running his White Rose Barber Shop on South George Street. He was a long-time smoker, and he had developed a gravelly voice. It was hard for family, friends and customers to understand him when he spoke. The local doctors sent him to Philadelphia to have surgery for throat cancer. The doctors in Philadelphia had to remove parts of his vocal chords. His voice didn't improve much after the surgery, and it became apparent that it was time for him to retire. He agreed, but only on one condition: that I would run his shop.

This created a difficult situation for me. I had worked for Frank Russo for about 3 years – and was very satisfied with my situation. If I stayed with Frank, Concetta's father would have to close his shop. It was a matter of family loyalty -- and of economic survival for the Randisi's.

Fortunately, Frank Russo understood my situation, and he supported my decision to leave. I was always grateful that we parted on friendly terms. I had helped his business grow, and now I had to strike out on my own to save my father-in-law's barber shop.

I retained the White Rose Barber Shop's customers – which included a cross section of neighbors, doctors, lawyers, businessmen and manufacturers. The customer mix was similar to what it was at Frank Russo's shop. I worked for Vincenzo on a commission, and the income was good.

Most of my customers talked, and I learned a great deal from them about how things were going in York. And, we would swap stories about the way York was before WW II. Because many of the customers were vets – we also told each other stories about our military service.

York had become a city in transition – with old industries moving away and new industries moving in. There were new suburbs being developed, and there were some troubling changes in the neighborhoods in York. The time came when people began to avoid coming into the city.

I had to do something to retain customers, so I got a variance from Spring Garden Township to relocate the shop to my house on Colonial Avenue. I had my garage remodeled into an attractive and modern shop. I named the new shop "Renda's Barber Stylist". It was only about 8 blocks from the White Rose Barber Shop on South George Street -- still close to most of my previous customers. They came to the new shop – together with many new customers from the neighboring Grantley campus of the York International Corporation. (This was the current successor name of the old York Manufacturing Company – where my father worked in the foundry with his friends and neighbors from Little Italy.)

York International had manufacturing plants, sales offices and service centers all over the world. Many employees in management were rotated to these remote sites. Whenever they came back to the home office for either sales meetings or reassignment, they would call me for a haircut appointment. Some just walked in with an appeal for a haircut. I saw some really bad haircuts, but I somehow worked these returning customers into the schedule.

I always felt glad to see them. They appreciated my work, and it felt good to be in demand. They told me horror stories of botched haircuts they had received elsewhere – often just before a meeting with an important customer. I had won prizes in several barber contests over the years and received compliments from customers and other barbers. Because of this, I knew that I gave an excellent haircut. As it turned out, I made the right choice in staying with barbering: I was good at it, the customers stayed with me, and I was happy in my work.

Note - The company is now a division of Johnson Controls, Inc. The business continues to expand - both in York and overseas.

CHAPTER 14

My Paintings

I want to mention that I continued my interest in painting throughout all the years I barbered. It began as a part-time hobby -- and grew into a continuing passion. Even today, people are amazed to learn that I am a self-taught painter. I still had the natural ability I demonstrated as a kid for sketching, and I just kept experimenting. I found that acrylic paints worked well for me.

During the 1960's and 1970's, hippie hairstyles with long hair were common. Many people did not get their hair cut for years. That left me, and other barbers, with fewer customers coming into our shops. I even studied for (and passed) the realtor's exam – thinking the slack times might never end.

There was a spare room in the back of the White Rose barber shop where I set up an easel. There, during the times without customers, I returned to my love of sketching and painting. I began to paint still life pictures and portraits. I began by copying photographs from the National Geographic and other magazines.

When I moved the shop to my house on Colonial Avenue, I also had a back room. I set up an easel and bench there and continued to paint. Fortunately, the pop hippie phase had faded, and customers came back. But, the desire to paint remained strong, and I was painting after hours and on weekends. Gradually, I began to paint military subjects.

In 1996, I painted a color rendering of Fred Folino in his Avenger. It showed his name on the fuselage – together with the Japanese flag decal for the recon plane he shot down with rockets. I superimposed a rocket on the decal just as the ground crew guys had done at Kadena – to clearly identify the Avenger as Folino's.

This personalized the Avenger – and commemorated his historic feat of being the first pilot ever to shoot down an enemy aircraft with unguided air-to-ground rockets. I sent a print of this painting to Fred. Unfortunately, he was in bad shape from some illness. His wife sent me a thank-you note that said he enjoyed the print very much. The years were beginning to catch up to the WW II pilots of VMTB – 232.

I also painted a color rendering of Joe Rosenthal's famous photo of the flag-raising on Iwo Jima. This iconic photo was originally shot in black and white. Subsequent attempts at colorized printing of this photo did not show the correct color of our Pacific Theater Marine uniforms. I think I captured the real "Pacific Marine Green" of our uniforms in my color rendering.

The CEO of York International Corporation saw the original painting in my shop one day while I was cutting his hair. He bought 30 signed lithographic prints for display in key York sales offices in the U.S. and overseas.

I donated a lithographic print to the US Marine Museum in Quantico, and they hung it in one of the display areas. Other prints hang in various sites in the York area – including the Office for Veterans Affairs.

On the occasion of the dedication of the York County Veterans Memorial in the city square in York on 30 JUL 2002, I presented a print of the Iwo flag-raising to General Jim Jones. He was at the time the Commandant of the Marine Corps. I got to talk with him only for a minute because he was suddenly called back to Washington to deal with some crisis overseas. But, he gave me a Marine token with his name on it before he left.

The local newspapers carried the announcement that Lt. Colonel Ollie North would be in York on 25 MAY 2004 to speak at a Junior League function at the Yorktowne Hotel. I went to the hotel lobby to see if I could get a minute of Col. North's time before he spoke. I had enjoyed his "War Stories" history program on Fox TV, and I wanted to present a fellow Marine with a signed print of my full-color rendering of the flag-raising on Iwo Jima.

I approached him and presented him with a signed copy of my print. He thanked me, and said it was so good he would have difficulty deciding whether to hang it in his office or in the FOX Newsroom studio. I happened to have a second copy with me, so I gave that to him also.

We were enjoying our conversation, mostly Marine talk, and we talked for several minutes more than we should have. He was very friendly and treated me with respect. The Junior League ladies were getting anxious about starting Colonel North's presentation, and we had to quit talking so that he could give his lecture on time. We said goodbye, and I was really glad to have talked with him. I didn't know what would become of the two prints.

A few months later, some of my customers began telling me that thcy occasionally would see one of my prints when the TV camera panned the newsroom at the beginning of the FOX News program. I have seen it on several occasions myself. I'm glad he kept his word, and I presume the other print is in his office.

Chapter 15

Post - WW II Echoes of the Red Devil Squadron, VMTB - 232

After I was discharged from the Marine Corps, I was able to stay in touch with the guys I served with in 232. There was a newsletter that came a few times a year to report happenings of the squadron members. There were often letters to the editor from squadron members who argued, “That’s not how I remember it.” in response to an article or letter in a previous issue. Also, there were reunions every other year to allow us to get together to swap tales of our wartime adventures in the Pacific Theater -- and to catch up on the current events in our lives.

I would write to the editor of the newsletter from time to time – mostly to add information regarding some item that had been reported in the previous issue. One time I sent several of the surrender leaflets that we had dropped on the Japanese forces near the end of the fighting. These leaflets gave instructions in Japanese as to what a Japanese soldier had to do to surrender. They also declared that those who surrendered would be treated well if they followed the instructions on the leaflet.

At other times, I sent copies of articles that appeared in the York papers whenever I was interviewed for a WW II story. One such story was about the time I delivered the telegram to the police station that reported the attack on Pearl Harbor.

There were also items in the 232 articles and newsletters about things that happened during the War that I did not know about at the time. Here are a few of these surprising after-the-War revelations:

Lee “Kit” Carson…No one in the Squadron believed Lee Carson when he said he was related to the real Christopher Houston “Kit” Carson. When we returned to the states for a 30 day furlough, Henneman, who was from the same Chicago area as Lee Carson, went to a local historical society and checked his story.

There, he found that Lee was in fact descended from the historical frontiersman, scout, soldier, and Indian fighter, "Kit" Carson.

And, years after that, I received an issue of the National Geographic magazine that included a photograph of the historic "Kit" Carson. Lee Carson had the same hair and facial features!

Bud Swartz…Bud was the guy who surprised me with his boxing skills when we were at the Ordnance school at Norman, OK. Later, as we were given our orders to ship out at San Diego, he seemed upset to realize that we were being sent overseas.

He failed to appear when we were boarding the troopship Sea Ray at San Diego. We never heard why he didn't show. Did he go AWOL – or was he excused for some hardship reason at home? Anyway, he never rejoined the squadron during our trip through the Pacific.

Shortly after the war, I was reading the sports page in a York newspaper. There was a story about a boxer who was killed in the ring in New York. It was Bud! It made me wonder how his life might have been different had he come with us. We volunteered to go in harm's way for our country, and most of us came home. He reappeared after the war and volunteered to go in harm's way in the ring – and didn't make it.

Vic Wagman…One day in the mid 1960's, a new customer who had just moved to York came into my shop for a haircut. He noticed a copy of the Marine publication "Leatherneck" in the magazine rack. He asked me if I had been in the service. I said yes, and told him I had been in the Marine Air Corps as an ordnance man for Avengers in the Pacific Theater. He said he had been in the Naval Air Corps – and served aboard the carrier U.S.S. Essex. He had been an ordnance man – serving carrier-based Avengers!

This was quite a coincidence -- our both serving as ordnance men for "Turkeys". Then he said that there was one mysterious happening that he had never figured out. One day during the battle for Okinawa, he recalled that the 2 squadrons of Avengers took off from the Essex – fueled and armed -- and were gone for 3 days and nights. He said he still didn't know where they had gone or what they had done during the time they were away.

I lowered my comb and scissors, looked at him and said, "I know exactly where they were. They were landing and taking off from the airstrip at Kadena to fly strike missions to support Marine ground forces. They did this continuously for 3 days and nights. I know, because the 232 Ordnance Group was assigned to rearm and refuel your Avengers for the 3 days they were assigned to assist with the invasion of Okinawa."

I told him that we were available to do this because our ground-based Avengers were not due to arrive at Kadena for 2 weeks. And, we knew how to arm Avengers -- and we had bombs and aviation fuel stockpiled near the airstrip. Someone had been smart enough to use our supplies to avoid depleting the bombs and fuel aboard the Essex: The Essex supplies were saved onboard and used for the pending carrier-based attacks against targets in Japan. This was an example of the type of inter-service planning and cooperation that helped us win the war.

We were both surprised to learn of our involvement with this handoff for the servicing of the Essex- based Avengers. Here, 20 years after the fact, we realized that our fingerprints may have been side by side on the bomb bay doors of the Essex Avengers during the battle for Okinawa.

Sam Hynes…During the research to confirm names, places and dates for my story, we looked in the book, "The War – an intimate history, 1941 – 1945" by Geoffrey C. Ward and Ken Burns. This is the book that accompanied the multipart video version of the same name that was shown on PBS television a few years ago. Ward and Burns are the script writer and film director of this acclaimed PBS television series.

In searching the book for details on the battle for Okinawa, we happened across segments of an interview with a Lt. Sam Hynes – who had been a Marine torpedo bomber pilot on Okinawa. Considering that there couldn't be that many Marine torpedo bomber pilots on Okinawa, we tried to remember if we knew of a 232 pilot named Sam Hynes. I could not recall the name.

But, just to check, we looked at my faded copy of the muster roll of Squadron VMTB – 232. It was dated May, 1945. On page 3, item 10 under "second lieutenant" (pilots) was the name "Hynes, Samuel L."

Had I known him? The officers and enlisted men did not usually mix on the airstrips. Their tent compounds were separate, and conversations between pilots and ordnance men were brief and confined to the requests and instructions necessary to keeping the Avengers flying with the correct bomb loads for each mission.

So, we Googled "Sam Hynes, WW II Marine pilot" – and found that he had written a book about his service in VMTB – 232! The title of his book is, "Flights of Passage: Recollections of a World War II Aviator." We got a copy of his book from the York County Library System. It includes stories of Lt. Hynes' adventures flying 232 strike missions. It also includes stories of Lt. Fox, Lt. Folino -- and other pilots. It was very helpful because it confirmed events, dates and places as I remembered them.

I also learned that Sam Hynes went to Princeton after the war on the G.I. Bill. He stayed to get a PhD in literature and joined the Princeton faculty. He had also written several other books.

The more I thought about him, the more I recalled the incident of the Japanese infiltrator who had been shot one night at Kadena. When a couple of us from ordnance were looking at the body of the infiltrator the next day, there were 2 Marine pilots there at the same time. Then, it hit me. One of their name tags read "Hynes". Yes, we had in fact met briefly at Kadena – but we didn't have a real give-and-take conversation about the infiltrator.

And, there's more: In looking at my back issues of the Squadron Newsletter, I see that Sam Hynes and I were both at the 232 reunion in Philadelphia in 1989. But, just like at the airstrips, the officers and enlisted men talked among themselves at the reunions. I guess this is human nature among units of comrades-in-arms having like assignments. Still, in looking back, I regret that there were wasted opportunities at these reunions to get to know and talk to others who fought together in common cause.

The Test of the Small Cask for Alcohol …
At the same squadron reunion in Philadelphia, I went up to Dr. Armbruster and said, "Sir, do you remember some of the guys bringing a drum of alcohol up to you on Okinawa and asking you if it was OK to drink?"

There were a lot of people standing around, and Doc was by nature a loud-spoken guy. He looked at me and bellowed, "That's a damn lie! No one ever brought alcohol to me to be tested!" But, I remembered the guys were drinking it. Someone must have taken a chance, bypassed the Doc, and guessed right. (Or, maybe Doc had forgotten the incident. It will remain a mystery.)

The Defusing of the 3 – 265 Pound Fragmentation bombs…
This story has an interesting follow-up. At the same Red Devil Squadron reunion in Philadelphia in 1989, there was a guy with the name "Carter" on his nametag. At first, I thought he was Fred Carter, the tail gunner on the para-pack drop mission I flew with Lt. Godbold.

So, I asked him if he had been a gunner. He said no, he had been a pilot. Then he asked me what my job had been. I told him I had been an ordnance man. He then asked me if I knew the name of the ordnance man who had defused the three 265 pound fragmentation bombs that had fallen from an Avenger at Kadena.

Before I could answer, he added, "That guy had guts." Then I said, "Yeah, I know who he is -- you're talking to him."

He looked surprised at my answer. Then I asked him, "Is the pilot who brought the bombs back and dropped them on the ground here tonight?" He laughed and said, "He's here tonight – but I'm not going to tell you who he is."

A little while after this conversation, I suddenly realized that *he* was the pilot, Lt. *George* Carter. Neither of us had recognized the other at first glance. After 44 years, he was still embarrassed by the incident. I felt honored to have been remembered by Lt. Carter with his compliment for my actions in a life-threatening situation.

I received a Navy Commendation Medal in 2002 – more than 50 years after I had defused the 3 fragmentation bombs. It came as a pleasant surprise to be recognized.

I have seen several stories in the local papers regarding long-delayed awards of medals. They usually say something like, "The paperwork was misplaced and delayed." So, I wasn't the only one who waited many years to receive my medal of merit.

The Last Bit of Shrapnel…I have included this item because of the time that had passed after the Japanese fragmentation bomb raid on Kadena in April 1945. During the raid, we dove into our foxholes, and a lot of guys got hit. I escaped – or so I thought.

50 years after that raid, I felt something catch on my undershirt while I was cutting hair. After I closed the shop for the day, I looked for whatever it was while I was washing up. The culprit was a tiny piece of shrapnel that had taken 50 years to work its way out of my chest!

A customer of mine who is a surgeon said that I was lucky. The shrapnel, though very small, had to work its way out from the area of my heart – narrowly bypassing some small arteries and nerves.

Norm Tabaka…When my father died in 1965, we invited people to come to our house after the funeral. My father was a kind and good man, and a group of 20 - 25 people had gathered at our house to express their sympathy and pay their respects to our family. Every chair was occupied, and people were sitting on the stairs.

Suddenly, someone said, "Let's have coffee!" I looked around and saw that we didn't have enough coffee makers to make the amount of coffee needed to serve everyone. Then, I remembered the times Norm made coffee for us in a big pot at our tent. He would put a one pound bag of coffee in the pot, and then heated the water with a little Coleman camp stove he got from the mess tent.

So, I got the biggest pot we had, filled it with water, poured in a pound of coffee, and brought it to a boil on our stove. Then, I slowly poured cold water into the pot in a slow, circular motion – just as I remembered Norm had done. The grounds sank to the bottom, and I ladled the coffee into cups. Everybody had coffee – and they all said it was the best coffee they ever had. Thanks, Norm.

Buddy Butera…

I have to mention Buddy here because he is still my friend. We graduated from high school together, we went to machine shop classes together, and we survived Okinawa together. At the age of 88, he still comes to see me to get his hair cut. And, he still works part time repairing orthopedic shoes at the premier shoe store in York!

The Universal Question…

Sometime after the war, my wife asked me, "Have you got any kids over there?" I said, "I can guarantee you that I don't have any kids over there. I wouldn't fool around with those women. They carried diseases that typically come with long-term poverty in Asia. And, they had probably picked up several STD's if they had served as "comfort girls" for the Japanese army of long-term occupation. That was enough to scare me off."

Shuri Castle…

Years later, I was talking to a guy at a meeting of the York County Marine Corps League who had visited Shuri Castle after the war. He said they had rebuilt it, and it was exactly as it was before the War. That must have cost a fortune. (I'll bet U.S. taxpayers paid most of the bill.)

Mario "Mike" Vecciarelli…

Mike Vecciarelli had put me in for a medal after I defused the 3 live bombs at Kadena airstrip. I knew he had been a sportsman and Golden Gloves boxer before War II, but I had lost track of him after the War. He died in January 2003 at the age of 89.

Norm Tabaka found Mike's obituary and sent it to Art Surtees at the Red Devil Squadron Newsletter. Art forwarded a copy to me – together with a copy of the eulogy his granddaughter Angela read at his funeral service. She included the story that – about a week before he died – Mike was eager to rejoin the Marine Corps.

He had been watching the news and had seen some footage of the developing wars in Iraq or Afghanistan. He insisted to his family that the Marines needed him, and that he was going to "ship out". The family played along and tried to talk him out of reenlisting. But, as always, he believed a man should fight for his country. He died of complications from surgery about a week afterward. He was always a good example of what it meant to be a Marine. Goodbye, Mike – and thanks for the memory. Semper Fi.

Major Alan Feldmeier…

Maj. Feldmeier's obituary appeared in the Red Devil Squadron Newsletter in March of 1993. He was 75. I knew he had joined 232 during the Solomon Islands campaign, and then he was our CO on Okinawa -- but I didn't know what he did after WW II.

The obituary said that he worked for the Strategic Air Command. While there, he was the developer of the "Buddy System" of air-to-air refueling between SAC bombers on strike-back patrol. This allowed planes to extend their range and time in the air during missions. This system was immediately deployed by SAC to keep their bombers aloft 24 hours a day during the long Cold War with the Soviets. Major Feldmeier served a vital role in keeping SAC bombers flying during what many call WW III.

I am proud to have served under him in the VMTB - 232 in 1945 -- the final year of WW II.

The 232 Reunion with 3 Generations of Rendas…

I had a wish to have my son Joe and his son Joey attend a VMTB-232 squadron reunion with me so I could have them see the camaraderie among the guys of 232. It came true in 2000 at the San Diego reunion. I took them with me, and they got to see and meet many of the survivors of the Red Devil Squadron that were my buddies during those tense and battle-filled days on Okinawa. These Red Devil Squadron vets were then mostly in their mid-seventies, and they were glad to meet my son and grandson.

In the afternoon, we toured the Naval Air Station at San Diego. We were allowed to walk among the jet fighters of the VMFA-232 Red Devil Squadron. They guys minding the jets invited us to climb up on the wings and check out the cockpits. Our designation was VMTB-232 – for Marine Torpedo Bombers. The new designation was VMFA-232 – for Marine Fighters, Attack. But, they were still Squadron 232, and they still bore the Red Devil insignia.

When we entered the reunion banquet that evening, the guys called out, "Here come the 3 Rendas." Toastmaster Art Surtees recognized us, and the group gave us an ovation. They had gotten to know us, and maybe we were the first family to attend with 3 generations.

Anyway, I got my wish: My son and grandson were exposed to the guys whom I had told them stories about over the intervening years. They had now seen them in real life, and I hope that they got a hint of the bonds we shared way back then – and still shared after 55 years.

Why was this so important to me? WW II was such a major event – and it affected the lives of so many who saw military service. I wanted them to get some in-person perspective of how real Marines interact when they get together. It's not the same thing as in history books or novels: There is a more human touch with face-to-face meetings. I was truly glad to have had this experience. I think it helped them to understand me – and the way I look at life.

Frank Renda's Pacific Voyages and Landfalls with VMTB-232, Aug 1944 - Nov 1945

Port of Departure	Port of Arrival	Days on Sea / Land	Key Islands on Route
San Diego, CA 08 AUG 1944	Espiritu Santo, (New Hebrides) 26 AUG 1944	18 / 30	Guadalcanal, Tulagi
Espiritu Santo Late SEPT 1944	Ulithi Atoll Late OCT 1944	30 / 120	Bougainville, Emirau, Peleliu
Ulithi Atoll 15 FEB 1945 (On Ulithi 3-4 mos.)	Okinawa 01 APR 1945	45 / 120	Iwo Jima, Leyte, (in the Philippines: 3 day stop)
Okinawa 15 NOV 1945	San Pedro, CA 30 NOV 1945	15 / home	Aleutians
Total days		108 / 180	

Discharged 30 JAN 1946

Doughboy Chapel on Ulithi: built by 30 U.S. Army volunteers in 30 days, 1944.

Doughboy Chapel on Ulithi, interior: All-coconut log construction visible.

Village maidens on Ulithi, dressed for the year-round 120°F plus temperatures.

Squadron VMTB-232 tent compound, in a coconut grove on Ulithi.

Maj. Alan Feldmeier, CO of VMTB-232, in the cockpit of his Grumman Avenger.

Native lizard of Ulithi, 4 feet long, climbing coconut palm.

Ordnance Group, VMBT-232. Author Frank Renda is in the front row, 6th from left.

Air Gunner Group, VMTB-232: turret gunners and rear gunner/radio operators.

Office Support Staff, VMTB-232, with the squadron scoreboard on Ulithi.

The author at the VMTB-232 tent compound on Ulithi.

A few Avenger pilots of VMTB-232 at mess on Ulithi.

The author's pup Judy. She was also the VMTB-232 squadron mascot on Ulithi.

W.O. Ratlitffe's dog, Lady - with the author's pup, Judy, at chow between two littermates.

A Grumman Avenger on Ulithi: The Avenger was the largest single-engine plane of WWII.

USO showgirls primping before a show on Ulithi. They were lost at sea on the departing flight.

Bob Crosby (Bing's brother) and the 5th Marine Division Band entertain the troops on Ulithi.

Burial of mystery disease victim Pfc. Tiedelbaum at the airstrip on Falalop Is., Ulithi.

Japanese planes downed on Okinawa. To clear the Kadena Airstrip, they were bulldozed into heaps.

Ack-Ack tracers from Yontan and Kadena airstrips firing at Japanese planes, 16 APR 1945. These attacks were a nightly occurrence all during April 1945.

Chow on Okinawa: At the entrance to the mess tent, Lee "Kit" Carson and the author are at the head of the line - facing the camera.

The author's Ordnance Assistant Willis Knight, with Judy 2, the author's Okinawa pup.

Eli Krueger with Avenger. Note tall landing gear, 13 foot prop, and open bomb bay doors.

View of Avenger's rearward-firing ball gun turret and the bottom gun pod. Both put the "sting" in the Avenger's tail.

The author (in truck) watching Okinawan refugees along the road fleeing from the fighting in the south.

The author, Don Neild and Gus Perilli exploring south of Kadena airstrip - on the road to Naha. Note rigid construction of the Okinawan wall.

Tech. Sgt. Mike Vecciarelli, Weapons Chief, VMTB-232.

The VMTB-232 Ordnance Group tent compound at Kadena airstrip.

The author's friend Vincent Kelly: He was killed on a "low-risk" mission by friendly fire - together with Lt. Fox, pilot, and an artillery spotter.

Eli Kreuger at a typical foxhole alongside a VMTB-232 Ordnance Group tent.

Marine guarding Okinawan tomb. These tombs were used by Marines as shelters during bombing and artillery shelling by the Japanese.

Eli Kreuger at typical modest dwellings in Okinawan villages.

Four Marines digging a foxhole at the VMTB-232 tent compound.

Full side view of an Avenger, with 2 Marines on the ground, showing the size of the plane.

The author (standing) and Bill Ashley with an ethnic Chinese family in Kin. They gave the family a ewe and a nanny goat - to provide milk for their children.

An ethnic Chinese family at their house in Kin.

The author, left, visiting an ethnic Chinese family in the town of Kin, Okinawa. The author and several Marine buddies brought them food.

Eli Kreuger at an Okinawan house.

Burial urns in a typical Okinawan tomb. Bones were placed in these urns. (The Okinwans were poor and had no objects of value to spare for burials)

An outside view of an Okinawan tomb having the traditional "keyhole" shape.

An Okinawan mother bathing with her children in a stream.

Okinawan women doing laundry for Marines. The washing machine was from the U.S. Navy.

Okinawan women of Kin washing their hair and sponge bathing at the communal pool

Okinawan women doing laundry for Marines. They sang the same song non-stop as they worked.

Don Neild, the author and O. L. Richardson in San Diego on their return from the battle of Okinawa.

Judy 2, on Okinawa - shortly before she was stricken with distemper.

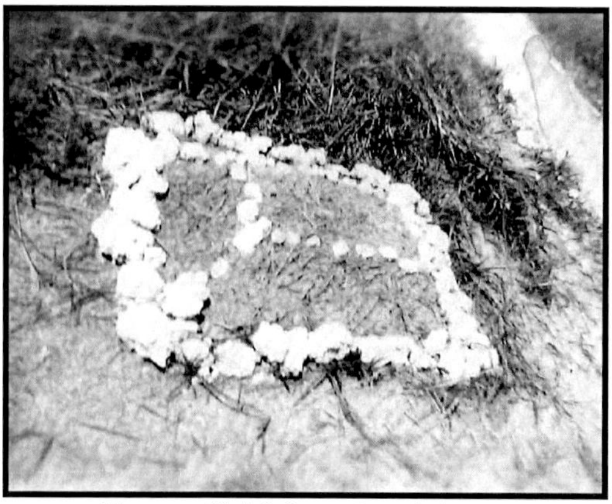

The grave of Judy 2. Decorating a dog's grave intrigued the Okinawans.

The ordnance delivery list for "mission strike number 80" by the Avengers of VMTB-232.

One of the thousands of Japanese planes shot down during the battle of Okinawa.

The townspeople of Kin at their communal pool on laundry day.

Typical Okinawan shacks on the edges of their villages.

Okinawans fleeing battlegrounds in the south - to seek refuge in the American areas in the north.

Eli Kreuger at the VMTB-232 compound with the insignia post. Note bomb trucks in the background.

The author's sketch of the beach at Guadalcanal - from the deck of the troopship Sea Ray, August, 1944.

The author's painting inspired by Joe Rosenthal's photo of the flag-raising on Iwo Jima, 23 FEB 1945.

The author with Col. Oliver North at the Yorktowne Hotel, 25 MAY 2004. He is presenting Col. North with a signed print of his color painting of Joe Rosenthal's iconic photo of the flag-raising on Iwo Jima, 23 FEB 1945.

Portrait of the author taken in York on furlough in JAN 1946.

VMTB-232 credit ledger (scoreboard) at the tent compound on Okinawa.

The author with Gen. James Jones, Commandant of the U.S.M.C., at the dedication of the WWII Memorial in York, 30 JUL 2002.

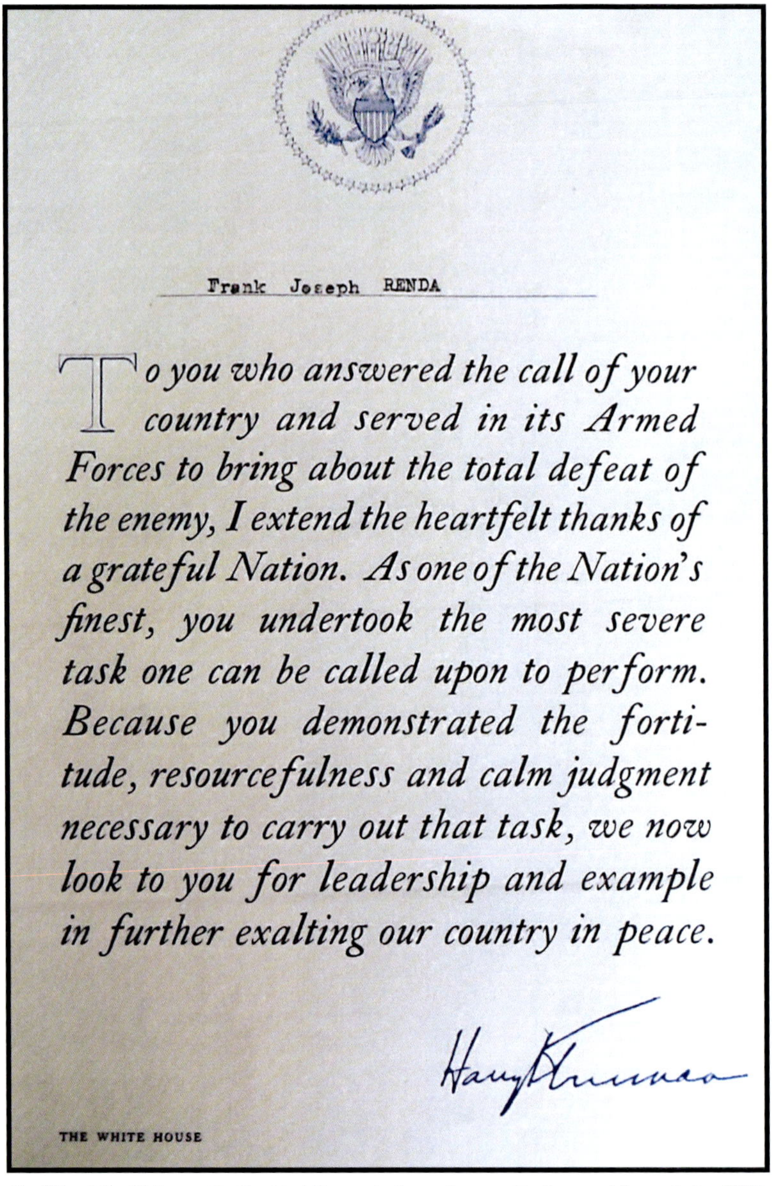

Frank Joseph RENDA

To you who answered the call of your country and served in its Armed Forces to bring about the total defeat of the enemy, I extend the heartfelt thanks of a grateful Nation. As one of the Nation's finest, you undertook the most severe task one can be called upon to perform. Because you demonstrated the fortitude, resourcefulness and calm judgment necessary to carry out that task, we now look to you for leadership and example in further exalting our country in peace.

Harry Truman

THE WHITE HOUSE

The "Thank You" letter sent by President Truman to those who served in the armed forces during WWII.

The author's oil painting of Lt. Fred Folino's Avenger - in recognition of the first-ever downing of an enemy plane by air-to-ground rockets.

Awards to VMTB-232, The Red Devil Squadron

Presidential Unit Citations

Campaign:	Dates:
Guadalcanal - Tulagi	07 AUG - 09 Dec, 1942
Okinawa - Ryukyus	22 APR - 14 JUL, 1945

Letters of Commendation:

From: R. J. Mitchell, Maj. General, U.S. Marine Corps, Commander Aircraft, Solomons
Citing outstanding efforts and successes in the Solomon Islands during the Campaign to halt and turn back the Japanese Advance.

From: Francis P. Mulcahy, Commanding General, 2nd Marine Aircraft Wing
Citing Close support mission strikes by VMTB-232, and Lt. F. F. Folino's downing of an enemy plane at night with rockets

Credit Ledger (Scoreboard) for VMTB-232, the Red Devil Squadron

1990-5-10
066/216

HEADQUARTER, FIRST MARINE DIVISION
FLEET MARINE FORCE,
c/o POSTMASTER, SAN FRANCISCO, CALIF.

August 31, 1942.

DIVISION DULLETIN)
: Commendation of Aviation Units stationed
NUMBER.....33a-42) at Guadalcanal, Solomon Islands during
period 21 to 30 August for results of aerial
operations undertaken during that period.

1. The Commanding General desires that all personnel of the 1st Division and attached units be apprised of outstanding efforts made by and the conspicuous successes attained by VSB-232, VF-223, VS-5 and 67th Fighting Squadron (USA), all of which were stationed at Guadalcanal, Solomon Islands during all or a portion of the 10-day period from 21 to 30 August, 19 42.

2. During this period one or more of the above named units have contacted the enemy on the sea or in the air eight times. Sustaining losses to themselves which were far below what might he expected in view of the results obtained they have destroyed 16 enemy twin-engined bombers, 5 single-engine bombers, 39 Zero Fighters and 3 destroyers in addition to which they have hit and probably destroyed one cruiser, two destroyers and 2 transports.

3. Operating under difficulties from an unfinished advance air base with limited facilities for upkeep and repair these units have without regard for the cost sought out the enemy at every oppertunity and have engaged him with such aggressiveness and skill as to contribute conspicuously to the success of the allied cause in the Solomon Island Area.

4. The Commanding General takes pleasure in conveying to the officers and men of the above named units in behalf of the officers and men of the 1st Division appreciation and felicitions for their outstanding performance of duty.

A. A. VANDERGRIFT,
Major General, U. S. Marine Corps,
Commanding.

DISTRIBUTION: All units.

Letter of Commendation to Squadron VSB-232 from Commanding Major General R. J. Mitchell, First Marine Division, 12 MAR 1944 for the service of VMTB-232 at Guadalcanal and the Solomons.

HEADQUARTERS OF THE COMMANDER AIRCRAFT, SOLOMON ISLANDS,
Care of the Fleet Post Office, San Francisco, California

March 12, 1944

From: The Commander Aircraft, Solomon Islands.
To: The Commanding Officer, Marine Torpedo Bombing Squadron Two Thirty Two
Via: (1) The Commanding General, First Marine Aircraft Wing.
(2) The Commanding Officer, Marine Aircraft Group Twenty Four.

Subject: Commendation.

1. As Commander Aircraft, Solomon Islands, I desire to commend the offiers and men of your ground echelon for their untiring efforts, their unselfish devotion to duty and their work, which of necessity was done under the most trying conditions. Their disregard of therir own peronsal safety during the shelling of the Bougainville airfields, in order that the aircraft assigned them could continue to operate, is worthy of the highest praise and admiration. It was their efforts that made possible the execution of the numerous air attacks made by the Torpedo Bombing aircraft of this command.

2. It is requested that a copy of this letter be made part of each officers' next fitness report and that a copy be placed in the service record book of each enlisted man concerned.

/S/ R. J. MITCHELL,
Major General, U.S. Marines Corps.

KV10/P15/rau (1334) 1st Endorsement 22 March, 1944
HEADQUARTERS, FMAW., FMF., C/O FLEET POST OFFICE, SAN FRANCISCO, CAL.

From: The Commanding Gneral.
To: The Commanding Officer, Marine Torpedo Bombing Squadron Two Thirty Two.
Via: The Commanding Officer, Marine Aircraft Group Twenty Four.

Subject: Commendation.

1. Forwarded with congratulations.

/S/ JAMES T. MOORE.

P15/kah 2nd Endorsement 29 March, 1944
HEADQUARTERS, MAG-24, FMAW., C/O F. P. O. San Francisco, Calif..

From: The Commanding Officer.
To: The Commanding Officer, Marine Torpedo Bombing Squadron Two Thirty Two

1. Delivered with consgratulations.

/S/ L. H. DELANO, JR.

3rd Endorsement 31 March, 1944.
VMTB-232, MAG-24, FMAW., C/O Fleet Post Office, San Franciso, Calif.

From: The Commanding Officer
To: The Officers and men, Ground Echelon, Marine Torpedo Bombing Squadron Two Thirty Two.

1. Delivered with congratulations.

/S/ ROLLAND F. SMITH

UNITED STATES MARINE CORPS
MARINE TORPEDO BOMBING SQUADRON-232
C/O FLEET POST OFFICE, SAN FRANCISCO, CALIFORNIA

19 August 1945

From: Commanding Officer.
To : All hands.

Subject: Commendation.

Reference: (a) Ltr CG, TAF to CO, VMTB-232, Serial: 0093, dtd 25May45.

1. Reference (a) is quoted in part below:

FMP/res
0093

HEADQUARTERS, TACTICAL AIR FORCE, TENTH ARMY
AND
SECOND MARINE AIRCRAFT WING

25 May 1945

From: Commanding General.
To : Commanding Officer, Marine Torpedo Bombing Squadron-232.

Subject: Commendation.

1. One month ago today Marine Torpedo Bombing Squadron-232 began flight operations in the Ryukyus area. Prior to 25 April, and since 4 April 1945, the ground echelon had been ashore at Kadena.

2. The flight operations of your squadron have been characterized by aggressiveness, intelligence, courage, resourcefulness and splendid professional skill on the part of your pilots. The execution of close support missions strikes, observation, night heckling and other dangerous and difficult missions have been the admiration of other flight personnel and the subject of much favorable comment and sincere appreciation by the ground forces. Lieutenant F. F. Folino's remarkable exploit in downing a Nip plane at night with rockets is one of the most unique military achievements of the present campaign. His exploit is matched in military effectiveness by mass and individual achievements in support of ground troops.

3. Not only your flight personnel, but your ground echelon too has contributed to the undoubted success of your squadron. The fine results your squadron has achieved are due in no small part to the splendid work of your ground personnel in all departments. The assistance they rendered to Marine Aircraft Group-33 and Marine Night Fighting Squadron-543, before the arrival of Marine Torpedo Bombing Squadron-232 flight echelon, is especially appreciated.

4. This commendation is addressed without prejudice to and in no way to take the place of higher award to which your squadron or yourself is or may later be eligible. I merely desire to let you know, at the end of your first months' operations, how much your work is appreciated and admired by all your comrades in this organization.

"Very well done to all hands in VMTB-232."

/S/ FRANCIS P. MULCAHY
FRANCIS P. MULCAHY

A. Feldmeier
A. FELDMEIER

Letter of Commendation to Squadron VMTB-232 from Commanding General Francis P. Mulcahy, Second Marine Aircraft Wing, 25 MAY 1945 for the service of VTMB-232 at Okinawa.

Awards to Frank J. Renda, Ordnance Group, VMTB-232

Clockwise from top left:

1. The Battle for the Phillipines Medal
2. Medal of Merit for defusing 3 bombs, Kadena Airfield, Okinawa
3. The American Theater Ribbon
4. The Victory Medal
5. A token of appreciation from Gen. Jim Jones for receipt of a print of the author's painting of the flag-raising on Iwo Jima
6. The Pacific Theater Ribbon

Airdrop leaflet, offering safe surrender to Japanese forces. Above: offer in English. Below: The reverse, message from front in Japanese.

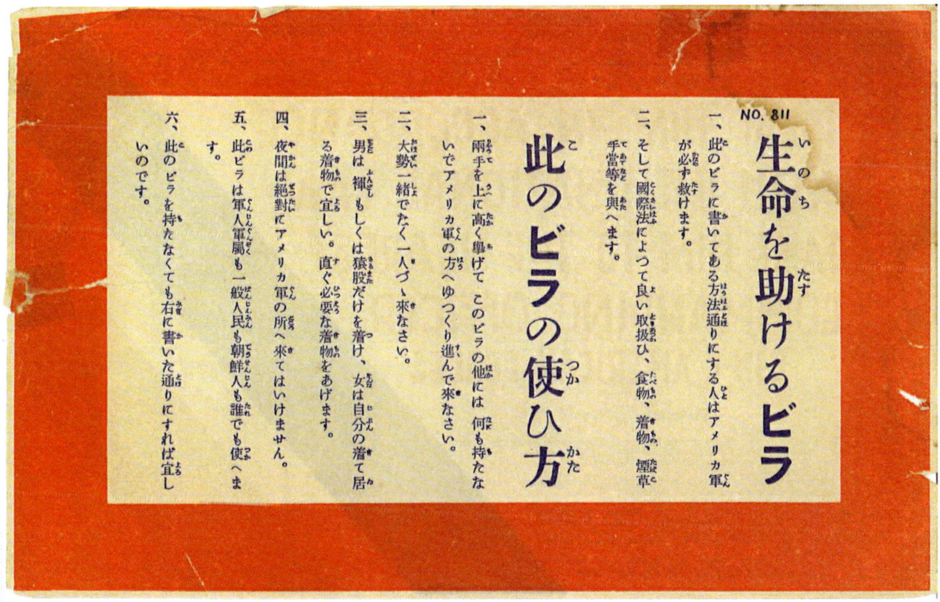

Airdrop leaflet, offering safe surrender to Japanese forces. Above: sketch of 2 soldiers carrying a wounded comrade on a stretcher. Below: the reverse with instructions in Japanese.

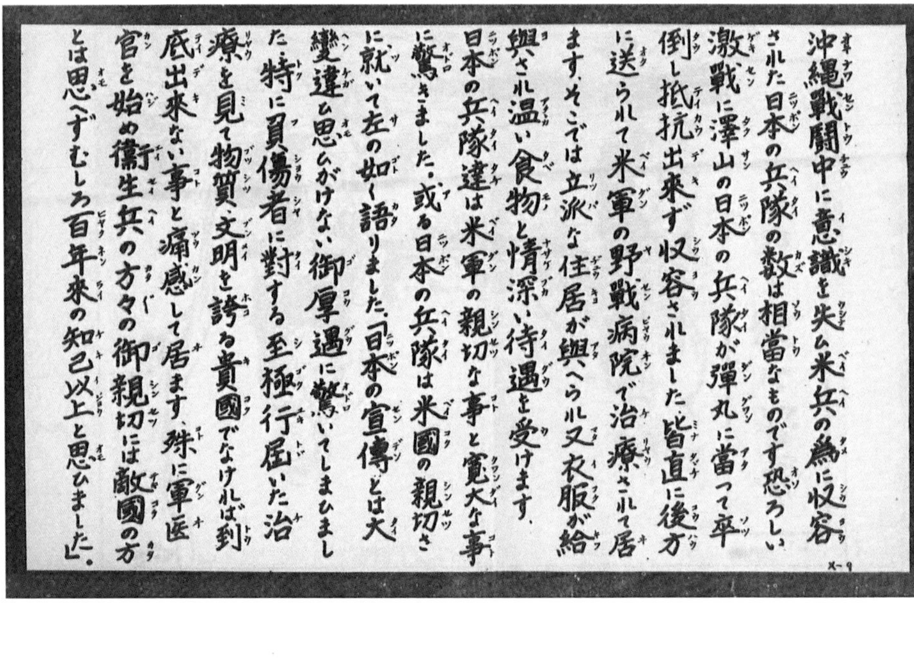
沖縄戰鬪中に意識を失ふ米兵の爲に收容
された日本の兵隊の數は相當なものです恐ろしい
激戰に澤山の日本の兵隊が彈丸に當って卒
倒し抵抗出來ず收容されました。皆直に後方
に送られて米軍の野戰病院で治療されて居
ます、そこでは立派な住居が與へられ又衣服が給
與され温い食物と情深い待遇を受けます、
日本の兵隊達は米軍の親切な事と寛大な事
に驚きました。或る日本の兵隊は米國の親切さ
に就いて左の如く語りました「日本の宣傳とは大
變違ひ思ひがけない御厚遇に驚いてしまひまし
た。特に負傷者に對する至極行届いた治
療を見て物質、文明を誇る貴國でなければ到
底出來ない事と痛感して居ます、殊に軍医
官を始め衛生兵の方々の御親切には敵國の方
とは思へずむしろ百年來の知己以上と思ひました」。
X-9

U. S. MARINE CORPS REPORT OF SEPARATION

NAVMC 78-PD.

CODE COLUMN

1. LAST NAME: RENDA, FIRST NAME: Frank, MIDDLE NAMES: Joseph
2. RANK: Corp
3. PAY GRADE: 5
4. SERIAL NUMBER: 903963
5. PERMANENT ADDRESS FOR MAILING PURPOSES: 136 S. Cherry Ave., York, Pa.
6. RACE: W
7. SEX: M
8. CITIZEN: YES x / NO
9. DATE OF BIRTH: 4Aug25
10. ADDRESS FROM WHICH PERSON WILL SEEK EMPLOYMENT: 136 S. Cherry Ave., York, Pa.
11. MARRIED: YES x / NO
12. NO. OF DEP.: None
13. PLACE OF BIRTH: Lonola, N.J.

RECORD OF MARINE CORPS SERVICE

SELECTIVE SERVICE DATA ▶ 14. REGISTERED: YES x / NO
15. ADDRESS AT TIME OF ENTRY INTO SERVICE: 136 S. Cherry Ave., York, Pa.
16. SEL. SER. BD. NO.: 3
17. COUNTY & STATE: York, Pa.
18. MEANS OF ENTRY: ENLISTED 2 / INDUCTED 1 / COMMISSIONED
19. PLACE OF ENTRY INTO ACTIVE SERVICE: RS, Philadelphia, Pa.
20. DATE OF ENTRY: 29Sep43
21. COMPONENT: REG. / RES. IIIB
22. PENSION CLAIM FILED: YES / NO x
23. PLACE OF SEPARATION FROM ACTIVE SERVICE: MCAB, Cherry Point, N.C.
24. DATE OF SEPARATION: 30Jan46
25. ORG. AT SEPARATION: MASU-1
26. TYPE OF DISCHARGE CERT.: Honorable
27. LENGTH OF FOREIGN AND/OR SEA SERVICE ⟶ YEARS 1 / MOS. 4 / DAYS -
28. MILITARY SPECIALTIES: Armorer, Aircraft (911P)
29. SERVICE SCHOOLS ATTENDED: Norman, Okla. — COURSES: Avn Ordnance — WEEKS: 14
30. PRINCIPAL MILITARY DUTY: Armorer, Aircraft (911P)

EMPLOYMENT AND NON-SERVICE EDUCATIONAL DATA

31. CIVILIAN OCCUPATION (TITLE): Engine Lathe Operator — D.O.T. NUMBER: 4-78 — NO. YRS.: 1/3 — LAST EMPLOYED: Aug43

JOB SUMMARY

Turned out brass bushings on lathe.

32. SECONDARY OCCUPATION (TITLE): - — D.O.T. NUMBER — NO. YRS.: - — LAST EMPLOYED: -
33. LAST EMPLOYER BEFORE ENTRY INTO SERVICE: C. Goodlings, Springdale Ave., York, Pa. — DATE LEFT: Aug43
34. JOB AID DESIRED: YES / NO x
35. EDUCATION IN YEARS: GRAMMAR 8 / HIGH SCHOOL 4 / COLLEGE - / DEGREE -
36. MAJOR COURSES: Vocational
37. TRADE COURSES: -
38. COURSES OF GREATEST INTEREST: Art, Mathematics
39. LAST SCHOOL ATTENDED: York High School, York, Pa. (1943)

PREFERENCES

40. PREFERENCE FOR ADDITIONAL TRAINING: Air Conditioning
41. JOB PREFERENCE: Air Conditioning and Refrigeration — REASON: Likes this work
42. LOCALITY PREFERENCE: York, Pa. — REASON: Home

I certify that all information on this form pertaining to the Naval Service of the above named individual is in accordance with the records of the U. S. Marine Corps and that a copy of this form has been delivered to him in person.

43. W. G. Van Buskirk — SIGNATURE OF C.O. OR PERS. O.

W. G. VAN BUSKIRK, Capt., USMCR — TYPE IN NAME OF OFF. - RANK

44. Frank J. Renda — SIGNATURE OF DISCHARGEE — DATE: 28Jan46

TO: HEADQUARTERS MARINE CORPS
Washington 25, D. C.

REDIFORM—PATD.—AMERICAN SALES BOOK CO., INC., NIAGARA FALLS, N.Y.

Report of Separation from the U.S. Marine Corps, for Renda, Frank Joseph, 28 JAN 1946. Includes employment and non-service educational data.

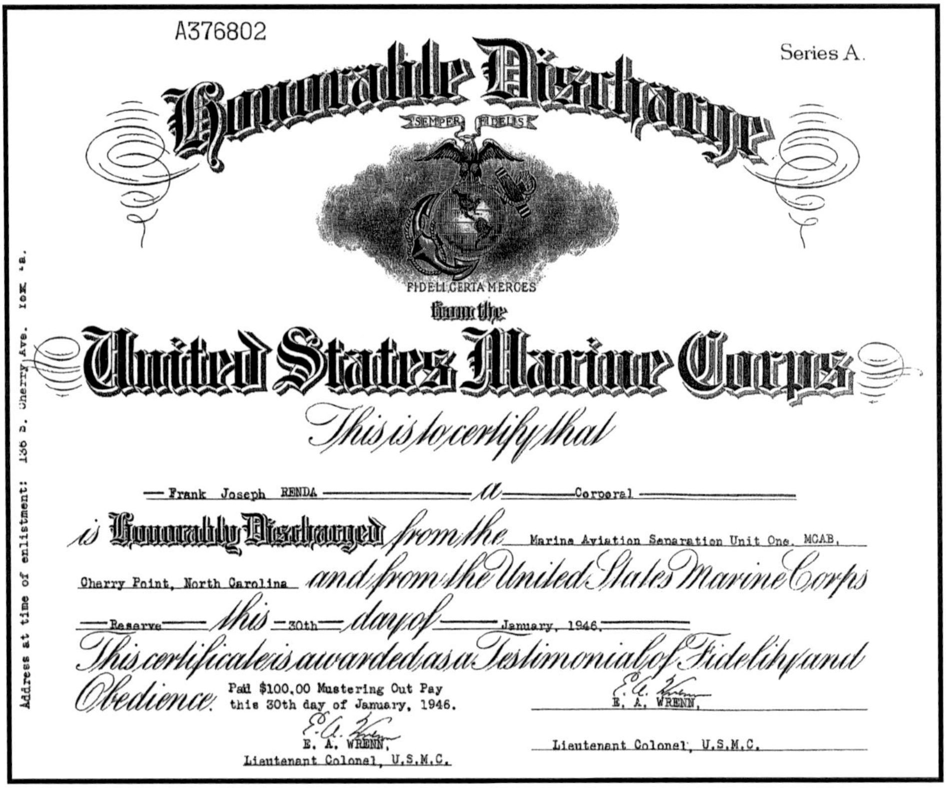

A376802

Series A.

Honorable Discharge

SEMPER FIDELIS

FIDELI CERTA MERCES

from the

United States Marine Corps

This is to certify that

Frank Joseph RENDA a Corporal

is Honorably Discharged from the Marine Aviation Separation Unit One, MCAB, Cherry Point, North Carolina and from the United States Marine Corps Reserve this 30th day of January, 1946.

This certificate is awarded as a Testimonial of Fidelity and Obedience.

Paid $100.00 Mustering Out Pay this 30th day of January, 1946.

E. A. WRENN,
Lieutenant Colonel, U.S.M.C.

E. A. WRENN,
Lieutenant Colonel, U.S.M.C.

Address at time of enlistment: 136 S. Cherry Ave.

Certificate of Honorable Discharge from the U.S. Marine Corps, to Frank Joseph Renda, Corporal 30 JAN 1946.

Certificates to Frank J. Renda from William Penn Senior High School and Atreus Wanner Vocational School, York, PA, in cooperation with York Industries for successfully completing:

1. *Sixty-three Hours in Blue Print Reading, 04 JUN 1946*
2. *Unit A in Machine Shop Practice, 04 JUN 1946*
3. *2,433 Hours in Machine Tool Operation, 26 NOV 1947*

These education classes were sponsored by the G.I. Bill.

Certificate

WILLIAM PENN SENIOR HIGH SCHOOL

and

ATREUS WANNER VOCATIONAL SCHOOL

YORK, PENNSYLVANIA

Co-operating with

YORK INDUSTRIES

This certifies that

FRANK RENDA

has successfully completed Sixty-Three Hours in BLUE PRINT READING.

This Certificate of accomplishment was issued on the 4th. day of June 1946.

YORK CITY SCHOOL DISTRICT

Superintendent of Schools

Director of Vocational Education

Coordinator of Vocational Education

Instructor

Certificate

WILLIAM PENN SENIOR HIGH SCHOOL
and
ATREUS WANNER VOCATIONAL SCHOOL
YORK, PENNSYLVANIA

Co-operating with

YORK INDUSTRIES

This certifies that

FRANK RENDA

has successfully completed Unit (A) in Machine Shop Practice.

This Certificate of accomplishment was issued on the 4th. day of June 1946.

YORK CITY SCHOOL DISTRICT

Superintendent of Schools

Coordinator of Vocational Education

Director of Vocational Education

Instructor

Certificate

WILLIAM PENN SENIOR HIGH SCHOOL
and
ATREUS WANNER VOCATIONAL SCHOOL
YORK, PENNSYLVANIA

Co-operating with

YORK INDUSTRIES

This certifies that

Frank J. Renda

has successfully completed 2,433 Hours in Machine Tool Operation.

This Certificate of accomplishment was issued on the 26 day of November 1947.

YORK CITY SCHOOL DISTRICT

Superintendent of Schools

Coordinator of Vocational Education

Director of Vocational Education

Instructor